LAW IN CONTEMPORARY SOCIETY

Law in Contemporary Society

THE ORGAIN LECTURES

VERN COUNTRYMAN

NORMAN DORSEN

ARTHUR GOODHART

LEON GREEN

MAURICE ROSENBERG

Introduction by Page Keeton

THE UNIVERSITY OF TEXAS PRESS, AUSTIN AND LONDON

International Standard Book Number 0-292-74606-7
Library of Congress Catalog Card Number 72-13848
Copyright © 1973 by *Texas Law Review*
All Rights Reserved
Printed in the United States of America

CONTENTS

ACKNOWLEDGMENTS

The authors acknowledge their indebtedness to the trustees of the Orgain Lectureship and to the School of Law and the Law School Foundation of The University of Texas at Austin. For permission to reprint the lectures, they are indebted to the editors of the *Texas Law Review,* in whose journal these papers were first published.

Norman Dorsen acknowledges the assistance in the preparation of his paper of John C. Gray, Jr., Daniel Pochoda, Nicholas B. Waranoff, and Peter F. Gold, sometime fellows in the Hays Program, and the thoughtful comments on an early draft of his colleague Professor Robert Pitofsky. He also wishes to thank Professor Roy Mersky of the School of Law of The University of Texas at Austin for his helpful suggestions.

Acknowledgment is due to Mr. Benjamin D. Orgain of Beaumont, and to the staff of the Tarlton Law Library of The University of Texas at Austin, for biographical details of the life of William Edmund Orgain. For editorial preparation of the collected lectures, the authors acknowledge the assistance of Professor Roy Mersky and Lance E. Dickson.

INTRODUCTION

The Orgain Lectureship was established as a memorial for William Edmund Orgain by his family and friends. It consists of a single lecture on a scholarly subject associated with the law, to be given annually at The University of Texas School of Law by a distinguished scholar.

William Edmund Orgain was born in Bastrop, Texas, in 1882. He attended Southwestern University for three years prior to transferring to The University of Texas, where he earned B.S. and LL.B. degrees. He was admitted to the bar in 1906 and, after spending a year as a member of the House of Representatives from Bastrop County, began the practice of law in Beaumont.

He was in succession a member of the legal firms of Parker and Hefner (of which he became a partner in 1908); Parker, Orgain and Butler; Hightower, Orgain and Butler; Wear, Orgain and Butler; Orgain, Butler and Bolinger; Orgain, Butler, Bolinger and Carroll; Orgain and Carroll; and Orgain, Carroll and Bell. And then, for more than twenty years, he was senior partner in the firm of Orgain, Bell and Tucker.

During this period he was active in land litigation, especially in cases involving the Spindletop oil fields and the Yount-Lee Oil Company. He was in every respect a "lawyer's lawyer." Oratory was not his forte, but his clarity of reasoning and cogency of expression in presenting his cases in a style and manner conveying his complete and utter conviction as to the rightness and justice of his cause were the qualities which gained for him the outstanding reputation that he so fairly earned. He never presented his legal argument until he had so simply and clearly stated the facts material to his theory of his case that it was difficult for an attentive listener to rationalize any legal result contrary to that for which he contended.

Unquestionably his success as a lawyer was grounded on his qualities as a man who genuinely loved his fellows and whose greatest interest was acting to rescue any he found in distress. He conveyed, as a man and as a lawyer, an impression of strength, vigor, and competence, a capability of coping with whatever problem arose. For those in trouble, he inspired the feeling that he was not only intensely interested in their problems, but had the time and ability to relieve the source of distress, whether he was assisting a young lawyer entangled in a difficult lawsuit or a churchman or educator faced with what appeared to be impossible funding problems.

His desire was to serve as a worker. But the quality of his efforts led him inevitably to leadership and to honors which he had not sought, and which he accepted with humility and as an opportunity for service. He was an able leader of the Jefferson County Bar, and one of a dozen outstanding and active laymen at the Methodist Church. His generosity and his efforts to help young lawyers were well known in the community.

A contemporary has described Will Orgain:

"*As a lawyer*, he was the finest I have ever known; to me he had no peer. In the first place, he possessed in full measure the two characteristics which every member of the law profession, in particular, should have—honor and integrity. Whether he represented a poor widow or a great corporation; whether he addressed a jury, a district court, or the Supreme Court—all could trust him. He had a phenomenal reputation for victory in the courts. Judges especially followed him because they had full confidence in both his integrity and the soundness of his side. One of our long-time district judges expressed it this way to me: 'I'm afraid not to hold with him—he will reverse me if I don't.'

"In the second place, he was one of those rare lawyers who possessed the two great talents so necessary in law, but so seldom found in the same lawyer. He could go into the library and do research in as fine and thorough a manner as any student ever did; then he could step from the library into the courtroom and try the case in a magnificent manner. There may have been some who could use more eloquent language in a jury speech, but no one could make a point quite so clearly, forcefully, or effectively, whether it be to a court or a jury.

"*As a man*, in his church and in the community, he was a leader. On many occasions, I have seen him unhesitatingly take his stand—always a wise, well reasoned, balanced stand, taken without rancor or malice, but strong and unequivocal. Other men followed his judgment—they seemed to want to know what he was thinking to help them make up their own minds, and I never saw him do or say a mean or little thing. He was a man's man in every sense of the word, but underneath his sometimes brisk, direct manner was a heart as big as all outdoors."

Another side of Will Orgain is described by an associate who frequently traveled with him to Longview on business:

"On all trips to Longview our invariable route was from Woodville due west to Corrigan, where we turned north toward Lufkin. The road between Woodville and Corrigan was a beautiful drive, due east and west, up and down hills, trees almost touching overhead with the road a narrow, single-lane blacktop. About twelve miles west of Woodville where a state park or rest area had been constructed there was a clear-water spring, flowing out of a hill just at the edge of the road. The spring was in its natural state and the whole area beautifully shaded by trees. Mr. Orgain and I never made this trip, whether going to Longview or returning, that we did not stop at this spring, kneel down beside it, and have a drink from the water flowing out of the hillside. One particular instance I will not forget. We were returning late at night, past midnight, going east, of course, in the face of a full moon which made the road truly 'a ribbon of moonlight.' Mr. Orgain was the first to suggest that regardless of the hour we stop and get our drink at the beautiful, clear spring, and so we did."

Upon this man Southwestern University bestowed an honorary Doctor of Laws degree, and in 1961 it named him as recipient of its Algernon Sydney Sullivan Alumnus Award for distinguished service to his fellow men.

He served as a member of the Texas Civil Judicial Council and of the Supreme Court's Committee on Rules of Practice and Procedure, and was president of the board of Southwestern University and vice-president of the Federation of Insurance Counsel. He was a member of the board of other institutions, including the American National Bank of Beaumont. Mr. Orgain also was a director of Gulf States Utilities Company. The company made generous contributions toward establishing the lectureship.

William Edmund Orgain died in Beaumont on November 20, 1965.

The first Orgain lecture, "Conflicting principles in English and American Law," was given in 1968 by Sir Arthur L. Goodhart, noted Anglo-American legal scholar. The second in the series was presented by Professor Leon Green of The University of Texas and entitled "The Law Must Respond to the Environment"; the third was by Professor Norman Dorsen of New York University School of Law on "The Role of the Lawyer in America's Ghetto Society"; the fourth was given in 1971 by Professor Vern Countryman of Harvard University on "The Diminishing Right of Privacy"; and the fifth was delivered by Professor Maurice Rosenberg of Columbia University under the title "Let's Everybody Litigate?"

From its inception in 1968, the Orgain Lectureship has established and maintained a high intellectual standard. The speakers have been eminent jurists, and the subjects on which they have spoken have been topical, controversial, and directly related to our contemporary society.

The quality and scholarship associated with the lectureship have led to an increasing interest in the series, which now receives the same acclaim and recognition that are enjoyed by other highly reputable and long established lecture series in the United States. The lectures are attended each year by a large audience and they reach a wider public through the medium of publication in the *Texas Law Review.*

Because of a repeated demand for copies of the earlier lectures, and particularly because the Orgain Lectureship has now completed five years of accomplishment, this was considered an opportune time to reprint the first five lectures in book form. While the lectures have no single unifying theme, they do present contrasting facets of our contemporary society as reflected by five great legal minds.

PAGE KEETON
Dean, School of Law
The University of Texas
at Austin

LAW IN CONTEMPORARY SOCIETY

Conflicting Principles in English and American Law

It is impossible to begin a discussion on conflicting principles of Anglo-American law with any talk of principles at all, for in its early stages our law was entirely lacking in principles. In this respect, the early English system stood in sharp contrast to its fellow system on the Continent, the civil-law system, which, because it was founded on the Roman codes, could be stated wholly in the form of general principles. The difference in the way the two systems were taught well illustrates this contrast. The Continental system was well suited to the formal lecture used in the European universities, for it enabled the lecturer to emphasize the general ideas with which he was dealing and to trace their logical development. Individual cases may have been used to illustrate the principles and to help in their interpretation, but the cases did not create the principles.

The early history of Anglo-American law teaching is entirely different. When Oxford, the earliest English university, was created at the beginning of the thirteenth century, there was no systematic law that could have been taught in a way similar to that of the Roman or Canon law. The common law was being made by the courts and by Royal ordinances. The process was almost the direct antithesis to that followed on the Continent because it began with the individual cases from which general rules could be developed. Much of the law came from custom, but custom is based on practice and not abstract reason.

ARTHUR LEHMAN GOODHART, K.B.E., Q.C., professor of law, University College, Oxford. Sir Arthur Goodhart was born in New York and educated in the United States (Yale) and Great Britain (Cambridge). He has been a visiting professor at Harvard, Yale, Virginia, and McGill universities, and has received honorary degrees in England, Scotland, Canada, Australia, and the United States. His publications include *Essays in Jurisprudence and the Common Law* (1931), *Precedent in English and Continental Law* (1934), *English Contributions to the Philosophy of Law* (1949), and *English Law and the Moral Law* (1953). In 1948 he was made a Knight Commander of the Order of the British Empire.

Thus the prospective barrister learned his law primarily by the practical experience he gained in attending the courts and in chambers. An attempt to put the common law in some order was made in 1268 by Henry Bracton, in his famous book *Leges et Consuetudines Angliae*, but his approach was entirely practical. Two centuries later, when the Inns of Court developed in London, a few lectures (called "readings") were held there, but again, these were of limited educational value.

Not until 1758 did a change take place in the teaching of the common law. It was then that William Blackstone became the first Vinerian Professor of Law in the University of Oxford, thus giving academic recognition to the teaching of this new subject. It was a stroke of good fortune that the first holder of this chair was gifted with literary genius in presenting and explaining this difficult subject because he was able to give it life. His lectures, *Commentaries on the Laws of England* (1765–1769), proved to be so popular that they hindered the teaching of law in English universities for nearly a century, for they contained most of the law that a prospective barrister then needed to know.

From the American standpoint, it was especially fortunate that Blackstone's lectures were published seven years before the American Revolution because many of the colonists found support in the *Commentaries* for their quarrels with the British governors and judges. In his famous address, "On Conciliation with America," Edmund Burke pointed out that over two thousand copies of the *Commentaries* were sold in a single year, even though Blackstone was a Tory.

Blackstone's greatest influence, however, was exerted after the colonies had become independent States. Because of the sudden unpopularity of things English at that time, the colonists were seeking to replace some of their English institutions; and the common law, already unpopular in the colonies because it was unsuited to the novel colonial conditions, was particularly vulnerable. Moreover, the common law proved to be easy to replace because it was so difficult to find; only a few English law reports were available in the American libraries. This was not the case, however, with the four volumes of Blackstone, whose recent popularity in America made them a handy substitute for the common law. Because they not only explained in the clearest terms what the law was, but also explained in a convincing way the principles on which the law was based, the *Commentaries* were able to play a dominant role in American legal history. The prospective lawyer was said to be "reading Blackstone."

The Blackstonian tradition, on which all law school lectures were founded both in England and in the United States was replaced in the United States around 1900 by the Harvard Law School case method introduced by Professor Langdell. Langdell's theory was that precedents, not principles, are the basis of the law, and therefore cases should be the chief means of legal instruction. This method reflected a cautious philosophy in that it repudiated ideas as a basis for the law because ideas might be dangerous. Instead it relied upon precedent, which, because it is based on the experience of the past, tends always to be conservative. This was in accord with the pragmatism of the period, a mood that may be attributed to the desire for stability that resulted from the radical changes wrought by the Industrial Revolution. During this period, one finds the House of Lords, the highest court in Great Britain, holding that it was absolutely bound by any precedent case that it had decided, even though the reasons for its conclusions were no longer valid, or had been wrong from the beginning. Similarly, the United States Supreme Court adopted a rigid interpretation of the Constitution at this time.

When the law has to deal with the changing problems of modern life, however, a pragmatic approach may be unsatisfactory. Modern conditions require that the law be based on general principles that are consciously developed to accord not with the past, but with newly developed needs. It is not surprising, therefore, that today both in the United States and in England much of the law is being reconsidered and reforms are being introduced. The Restatements of American Law, now being published by the American Law Institute, do not purport to present a new code, but they inevitably will result in a more logical and effective legal system. Similarly, the recently created Law Commission in England will attempt to codify as far as possible both the common law and the statutory law.

I. Constitutional Law

The English and American constitutions resemble each other in a limited number of ways: Both provide that voters be given an opportunity to vote from time to time for representatives to the legislature, and both provide that judges be independent; but this is as far as the comparison goes. In a sense even these constitutional similarities do not exist, because the British constitution is not a written document. It can be stated in six words: "The Queen in Parliament is supreme."

The Queen's role is based on an anachronism requiring her to say, "La Reine le veult" whenever Parliament has enacted a bill in proper form. A statute formalized in this manner is absolutely binding on all judicial and executive officers, however unjust or unreasonable it may be.

It is possible for an unwritten constitution, with all the sovereign power concentrated in a few hands, to succeed in Great Britain because it is a small country with strong bonds of history and national tradition and no strong conflicting religious, economic, linguistic, or racial differences. The United States, on the other hand, with its vast expanse, its racial differences, and its conflicting territorial interests, requires a more rigid system with the powers divided according to certain fixed rules and with the limitations on government stated in written rules that are binding and enforced by the courts. The absence of a written constitution in England does not mean, however, that there are no limits on government. The limitations on government in England are found in certain standards that may alter gradually from time to time. The reliance on standards to provide limitations on government can be illustrated through the concept of "due process" as it operates in England.

Due process means a fair trial, and in both England and the United States the adversary principle is central to the concept. A fair trial is a contest between the opposing parties, who in most cases are represented by counsel. The fairness of the contest depends upon three essential elements that are for historical reasons more clearly recognized in England than in the United States.

The first essential is an able and upright judge. Because the judge plays the part of a referee or umpire, he must be unprejudiced; otherwise the judicial process would be a sham. The authority of the whole legal system depends in large part upon the respect accorded the judge in England. When the King's judges travel round the country on circuit administering the Royal justice, they are entitled to Royal honors. Whenever they come to an assize town, they are met by the High Sheriff of the County, and trumpeters blow a fanfare. There is a story that some years ago two judges, who were holding the assizes at Oxford, dined at All Souls College. At the end of the dinner the Warden proposed the Queen's health. When the junior Judge, who had been appointed only recently, rose to his feet to join in the toast, the senior Judge pulled his coattails and said in a hoarse whisper, "Sit down, you fool. *You* are the Queen!"

Unfortunately, this respect for the judge has not been as great in America as in England, owing in part to an historical accident. In England the judge, although the King's representative, insisted on complete independence, especially after the last of the Stuart kings, James II, fled to France. Colonial judges, however, were unable to maintain this independence in America because the colonists regarded them as representatives of the British government enforcing alien laws. This attitude resulted in a diminished respect toward judges which continued to some degree after American independence was established. The Jacksonian period, with its denigration of all public officers, also contributed to the antijudicial tradition that has only recently come to an end in almost all the States.

The second essential element in a fair trial is a responsible bar controlled by strict professional standards. Here again the English bar has been fortunate in its history. Since the fourteenth century, a future barrister in England has been required to join one of the four Inns of Court. Here he must dine from time to time with his fellow members and study the law. After he has passed his examinations, he is called to the Bar by his Inn in a ceremony that emphasizes in part the strong bond of fellowship which he has with other members of the Inn. This social bond with other members of his Inn continues throughout a barrister's professional life and is of major importance in maintaining a high standard of professional behavior. Besides this informal code of behavior that members enforce upon themselves, the Benchers, who constitute the governing body of the Inn, also have the power to disbar any member of the Inn for any grave offence, subject to an appeal to the Judges. Disbarments of this sort, however, are exceedingly rare.

The duties of a barrister in England go beyond his allegiance to his client, and these high professional standards are central to the English concept of "due process." This is well illustrated by a comment of the Lord Chief Justice, Sir Alexander Cockburn, made in 1864:

> The arms which an advocate wields he ought to use as a warrior, not as an assassin. He ought to uphold the interests of his clients per fas, not per nefas. He ought to know how to reconcile the interests of his clients with the eternal interests of truth and justice.

It was inevitable that equally strict standards would not be applied to the various state bars in the United States. In the first place, the greater number of lawyers in the United States makes strict standards difficult to enforce. Secondly, the traditions and standards that play such an important role in group behavior in England are less effective in the United States because American lawyers are not closely organized. Fortunately, a new spirit of companionship seems to be developing rapidly in most of the bar associations so that the old concept of uncontrolled independence is being replaced by the standards of association. The strongest unifying force in the American legal system has been its great law schools, which are unique in legal history. In many ways they perform the same functions that the English Inns of Court have done during the past centuries.

The third essential element of a fair trial is an impartial jury, which in the United States is guaranteed by the Constitution. The explicit constitutional requirement of a trial by jury may explain why so much time and effort is spent in choosing an American jury, with the result that impartiality is regarded as being almost synonymous with lack of intelligence because a prospective juror may be challenged if he has formed any ideas that could remotely affect his verdict.

II. THE CRIMINAL LAW

In criminal law and its procedure, the contrast between the two systems may be said to derive directly from the difference between the strictness of American rules and the flexibility of English standards. For example, the federal constitution provides that no one shall be forced to give evidence against himself; at first sight this would seem to be a clear and precise statement, but the large number of recent cases shows how uncertain it may be in application. Is a blood test evidence? If an accused person is questioned for forty-eight hours, does this constitute compulsion? Is the rule violated if a statute provides that an accused person who pleads guilty will receive a lesser penalty than if he is found guilty after a trial? In America, these questions are answered by attempting a strict compliance with the mandate of the Constitution. In England, on the other hand, similar questions arise, but the trial judge is given a certain discretion to decide whether the standard will be applied in a particular case.

A substantive criminal-law question that is of major importance and arises frequently in both countries concerns the strictness with which crimes shall be defined. It is argued on the one side that no one ought to be held criminally liable if there is any question concerning the criminal nature of the act. For example, it would be improper to provide that any "dishonest" act constitutes a crime, as the concept of dishonesty is too vague. On the other hand, it is said that this is a question of degree so that a person who does an act that a reasonable man would recognize to be wrongful cannot complain if the courts hold that it has fallen on the criminal side of the line. In England, a law that attempts to define the crime of theft in terms broad enough to cover the present conglomeration of crimes relating to dishonesty has recently been enacted. Theft is defined as "the dishonest appropriation of property belonging to another with the intention of permanently depriving that other of it." American legislatures, because they are more reluctant to extend judicial power, may be hesitant to introduce such broad definitions in the law.

III.   THE LAW OF TORTS

The development of the law of torts has followed closely parallel lines in the English and American systems. In general terms, the law of torts is concerned with the right of a person who has been injured to recover damages from another whose act or failure to act has caused the injury directly or indirectly. At first sight, it seems reasonable to base liability upon the principle that he who harms another ought to be liable for the consequences. Such a strict principle, however, would make the risks of ordinary acts in society so high in terms of liability that it would have a suffocating effect upon our freedom of movement. It is doubtful whether even early society had such a strict rule in regard to all acts, although where land was concerned, the law of trespass imposed absolute liability upon anyone who entered another person's land, even if the entry was made in the reasonable belief that it was lawful. This was the most efficient method of determining title to land, and it is still the law.

In trespass to the person, the rule was less strict because in these cases both parties might have been acting when the accident occurred. As society became more complex with the start of the industrial and transport era, it became necessary to devise a way to allocate the burdens of responsibility for the injuries that occurred in society. At the beginning of the nineteenth century a new approach was found in the action for negligence, which is now by far the most important tort action in both England and the United States. The reasonable man became the dominant figure in the law of torts, and a modified form of the doctrine of mens rea was introduced. The ability to foresee became the most important characteristic of the reasonable man because, if he could not foresee that his act might injure another, then there was no reason why he should not act, and hence, no liability.

This foresight doctrine, although satisfactory in most instances, required some limitation because the burden imposed through the use of the doctrine might be too harsh in certain circumstances. The concept of "duty of care" was therefore introduced. It provides that a man cannot be held liable in negligence unless he has violated a duty of care, this duty usually being limited to the direct and immediate consequences of his act.

This duty of care based on reasonable foresight, however, has proved to be too narrow in certain instances, especially in accident cases. Crowded conditions of modern life and the helplessness of the consumer has caused the duty to be extended in products liability cases. This extension was first recognized in American law in the case of *MacPherson v. Buick Motor Company*, and it has been followed in Great Britain in *Donoghue v. Stevenson*. The duty of care based on reasonable foresight may also prove to be too narrow when a potentially dangerous situation has been created. Thus, an occupier of land may be liable to his neighbors if a water reservoir bursts its banks even though he himself has taken reasonable care to prevent such an accident. The scope of this principle, however, is uncertain in both countries.

In the United States a new school of thought favouring the insurance principle is beginning to develop, but it has not as yet received much support in Great Britain. This would do away with the idea of fault in regard to those accidents in which social justice demands that the loss fall on the employer or the owner because they can regard the accident as part of the cost of business and can insure against it. It is probable that a modified form of this idea will be applied to motor accidents in the near future.

IV. THE LAW OF CONTRACT

It is strange that the principle on which the law of contract is based is still uncertain both in the United States and in England. Although the English judges before the sixteenth century knew of the Roman-law doctrine of a contract as an agreement based on a meeting of the minds of the contracting parties, this concept was not imported into the common law. The common-law contract, which was a development from the law of torts, was based on the promise given by the promisor to the promisee with the knowledge that the promisee would rely on it, and that the breach of the promise might cause him damage. No actual meeting of the minds of the two parties was necessary because a promisor would be held liable for a breach of the promise if a reasonable man would interpret the promise in a sense that the promisor never intended. Reliance of the promisee is what made the promise effective. Evidence of reliance was found in the consideration that the promisee gave to the promisor in return for his promise.

At the end of the eighteenth century and during the first half of the nineteenth century, the English courts inclined toward the French doctrine that a contract must be an agreement between the parties, but under the influence of Professor Williston at Harvard and Sir Frederick Pollock at Oxford the promise doctrine has now been generally accepted. The question is more than merely one of semantics because it affects the law relating to mistake. Under the promise doctrine, for example, a promise is binding even if it can be proved conclusively that the promisor made an error and would not have made the promise if he had known the true facts. Both the English and the American laws have hitherto refused to accept the continental doctrine of abuse of rights. A promisor is strictly bound by his promise and cannot plead that a change in conditions has made it unfair for him to be asked to perform his promise.

V. The Law of Real Property

Although the subject of property seems to be based entirely on technical rules and not on principle, the history of the law of property shows that this is untrue. In medieval times land was almost the only source of wealth. It was also the basis on which the family was founded. As a result, family settlements were of the utmost importance. Since there were so few transactions, long and complicated documents of title were not burdensome. No attempt to simplify the law was made until the beginning of the nineteenth century, and not until the twentieth century did the registration of title became important. Today the English law of property no longer places such an exaggerated emphasis on the protection of title, but still it is more complicated than American property law and makes the transfer of title more difficult.

VI. Procedure and Evidence

Because the areas of procedure and evidence cover so wide a field, it is necessary to confine remarks in this observation to the main criticisms found in each country.

In the United States, the chief criticism is that of delay. In the criminal courts delay is due in large part to a desire to take every procedural precaution to avoid the possibility that an error will be made and an innocent man unjustly punished. This desire for perfection, however, may be self-defeating. A trial may be delayed by the inordinate time occupied in choosing a jury; then, the giving of evidence is delayed by innumerable objections to the introduction of evidence on various technical grounds. If the accused is convicted, there may be a large number of appeals in the state courts, followed by entirely separate actions in the federal courts based on the ground that the trial has violated the Constitution in various ways. The civil courts are also open to criticism for the delay caused by overly technical procedural and evidentiary rules. Attempts to improve the practice have been made through the development of pretrial procedural devices, but this has not proved to be as successful as had been hoped.

The main criticism of the English procedure is based on the excessive costs that a losing party may incur. Strenuous efforts have been made to reduce these, but they have achieved little success. The English rule that the successful party may recover all the costs he has reasonably incurred, including the fees he has paid to his own lawyers, is largely responsible for this problem.

VII. Conclusion

Shakespeare, who was no mean lawyer, said that "comparisons are odorous." It is true that comparative law may prove to be dangerous if it causes one system to be overly ready to accept a rule or a principle that has been found to be successful in some foreign system without realizing that the conditions in which they operate may be different. On the other hand, there is a strong justification for the study of comparative law. The light that such a study may throw on one's own legal system may sharpen one's critical sense when he suddenly discovers that a rule he has always regarded as axiomatic has been rejected in a foreign system. Nowhere is this more true than in a comparison of the English and American systems, because they are so tied to one another in background. Yet, because of differences between the two countries in population and geographic size and in the composition of their societies, and occasionally because of accidents of history, they contrast significantly in many areas of the law.

The Law Must Respond to the Environment

LEON GREEN

My discourse is developed around the swift movement of the environment, the multiplications of powerful groups, the importance of these groups to the individual, the problems created by the abuse of group power, and the responsibilities these groups impose on lawyers in the making and the administration of law.

I

The swiftly moving environment may be visualized by a few examples. What has happened to the railroads built in the latter half of the 1800's, built by gifts of federal and state governments of hundreds of millions of dollars in cash, by other millions invested by private citizens, by vast grants of land with bountiful natural resources (in Texas alone an area the size of Alabama), and by thousands of laborers who gave their lives and limbs for which neither they nor their families were compensated? They opened our undeveloped national domain and made possible hundreds of highly productive enterprises that laid the groundwork for an affluent and powerful society.

Aside from moving about half of the freight tonnage of the coun-

LEON GREEN, professor of law, The University of Texas. Leon Green was born in Oakland, Louisiana; his degrees are B.A., Ouachita College (1908), LL.B., The University of Texas (1915), M.A. (hon.), Yale University (1928), and LL.D., Louisiana State University (1938). He was admitted to the Texas bar in 1912 and practised law in Austin, Dallas, and Fort Worth. His appointments have included professor of law and dean of the School of Law, University of North Carolina (1926–1927), visiting professor of law, Yale University (1927), and professor of law and dean of the School of Law, Northwestern University (1929–1947). His publications include *Rationale of Proximate Cause* (1927), *Judge and Jury* (1930), and *The Litigation Process in Tort Law* (1965). He is co-author of *Cases on the Law of Torts* (1968) and compiler of *Injuries to Relations* (1949). He is a member of the Texas, Connecticut, Illinois, and Chicago bars.

try, what is the significance of the railroads today? Where are the accommodation locals, the trolleys and interurbans, the flyers, chiefs, cannon balls, rockets, streamliners, limiteds, and zephyrs, with their long trains of mail, express, coach, pullman, parlor, diner, and observation cars? Where are the little depots and the grandiose stations; the passengers with their families, guests, and neighbors who crowded them every Sunday and holiday? How many of us were there and felt our pulse quicken as the throbbing locomotives applied their power and began their departure, or felt the thrill of a passenger as the click of the car wheels increased and the train reached the peak of its rhythmic speed?

What has happened to the railroads in the short period of one lifetime has also happened to almost everything that people control in the physical world—architecture—home furnishings—machines and tools —preparation of foods—personal dress—methods of entertainment— variations numberless in designs and functions, important for the moment but destined only to mirror how everything comes and goes at great speed and other things take their place for an instant—a fleeting mirage that we give little more attention than we give the whirling of the planet that holds us in our places.

Do ideas also come and go; live awhile, grow pale, and die; the great abstractions: religions and their ceremonials—morality and ethics —economic theories—scientific speculations—philosophies—government and law? Here also is great movement—rarely sharp and swift— usually with glacier speed over long periods of time. In government and law, for example, once a basic pattern is established, ideas in their development differ from those that produce most physical creations in that they have a longer period of gestation and greater infant mortality; if they survive, they gain wide acceptance slowly and are difficult to uproot after they die. Yet even here speed is deceptive. How many times have the teachings of Socrates, Plato, Jesus, and other great law-givers and teachers been reinterpreted—filled with meanings more congenial to later societies?

You will recall how slowly it seemed some of the institutional ideas we now consider basic to our society became acceptable to those of our day—public schools and universities—income tax—labor unions —votes for women—child labor laws—reclamation and conservation of natural resources—federal reserve bank and guaranty of bank deposits—regulation of public utilities—workmen's compensation and employer liability acts; more recently—civil rights on many fronts—

school integration—federal aid to education—fair employment and minimum wage—open housing—food and drug acts—old age assistance—social security—medicare and other important measures of this century designed to advance and protect the lives and rights of people.

The same is true of the ideas designed to make the administration of the courts responsive to social and economic developments—the administration of law and equity under a single system with responsive rules of civil procedure—the integration of state bars and the administration of state courts under rules fashioned by the courts—the necessity of a code of ethics, law schools, and institutes of continuing legal education.

II

As a by-product of the extended struggles to establish and maintain our social order we learned that individuals can multiply their power many times by combining their efforts. This has resulted in the transformation of what was considered by some a society of individuals into a group society. Today the translation of any important idea into action must await group organization. The individual does his work, meets his responsibilities, gains his status, receives his protection under the shelter of the groups of which he is a member, through their functions attains his highest powers and satisfactions, and renders his greatest services to his fellow beings. Also, it is under the restraints of the group that he develops his self-restraints.

The individual surrenders some of his freedom to every group by which he is accepted; he mortgages freedom for recognition and security. It is here also that his personal dignity is achieved, respected, and applauded. Give him the key to his cell, the run of the establishment, and his cup runneth over. The individual without group identity is outside looking in—his freedom a penalty few can afford or endure.

Is freedom what we desire, or do we hunger for the ties to others that obligate us to strive for the full development of our powers—perhaps also to share the fruits of their powers?

If group life is essential to the development and growth of the individual, could it be that we have talked and taught too much about our freedoms and rights and thought too little about our allegiance and obligations? Freedom uncontrolled in its destructive power is not unlike the release of the power of the atom—each must be kept under severe restraints and that is why no civilized man or group can be wholly free. That is why in the processes of education restraints in the uses of power are equally as essential as in its development. Fortunately for most of us the very pressures of group society negate much of our teachings about rights and freedoms. Unfortunately for some, this is not true, and we have young people and some not so young, in our public schools, colleges, and universities, and drop-outs along the way, whose ideas of freedom and rights are abnormally perverted— their sense of obligation and allegiance to the groups that have nurtured them, nonexistent. We think of them as delinquents, freaks, perverts, radicals, rebels, and even as criminals, when in fact they are the victims, sometimes the waste, of a group society that has not yet fully realized that many of its problems arise from a mythical philosophy of rugged individualism that rejects group respect and responsibility.

But if group life is essential to growth and development of the individual—the richness of his life dependent upon acceptance by others to whom he is willing to give his allegiance—think what must be the despair and bitterness of those who are denied acceptance. Is this power to reject and deny those who seek its fruits what we mean by a free and open society? Are its groups under no obligations to those who offer their support and allegiance? How else than by acceptance can the wretchedness of resentment and injustice be avoided? What other base can be found for freedom, equality, and loyalty?

The multiplication and remultiplication of groups within groups with their countless interrelated activities generate tremendous social power. They also create serious problems for government and law. When directed by the irresponsible and lawless, group power is frightening. It is even more frightening when held in excess and directed to the ends of highly respected groups at the expense of other groups, a community, a state, or even a nation.

What justification can be found for a teacher's union closing the schools of a great city; a teamster's union cutting off the fuel supply of the city's inhabitants; a small group of legislators blocking a vote on some vital measure sought to be enacted into law; the excessive hiking of prices by processors of some product essential to the health or economy of a nation? If respectable groups by virtue of their raw power can force the acceptance of their terms, what answers have we to groups with no power to achieve their demands except violence and threats of violence?

No other society was ever so dependent on so many powerful groups. Consider those who control the instruments of communications and transportation by land, sea, and air; the money resources of banks and insurance companies; the oil, steel, electric power, drug, tobacco, and lumber companies; the networks of trade associations and formidable labor unions. However out of social focus their actions may be, they are under slight controls or restraints except their own—their power for both good and evil immeasurable. How much they have strengthened or weakened, advanced or thwarted the development of the social order by the excessive exercise of their power can never be known. But there is no doubt that the shift of the social center-of-gravity to groups powerful enough to challenge the institutions of community, state, and nation presents many problems.

How long the social order can withstand this shift to groups that possess and occupy these strategic strongholds of power or can be sustained on a base of undemocratic groups; or whether the social order itself has been transformed into a league of powerful baronies, each a law unto itself; and finally whether a balance-of-power through political diplomacy setting group over against group, can be relied on to neutralize their power, present problems insoluble by debate and which we shall probably have to live with from now on out.

III

What relevance do these problems have for the lawyer and his profession? The lawyer does not have to be told that government and law must respond to the environment. He lives and does his work on small and large scale in that climate. He knows how the environment may be convulsed—in fact is constantly convulsed—by the events of the day—the emergence of the automobile—airplane—telephone—television—credit system—computer—supreme court decision—industrial strike—new drug—new source of power, or by great tragedies—depressions—riots—racial conspiracies—wars—assassinations; how these convulsions strain the fabric of the social order and require readjustments throughout the governmental structure—the setting up of new procedures—extensive repairs to existing law and the making of much new law. It is at this point that the lawyer's power plays such an important role. Of all his fellow professionals he is the most involved.

The lawyer's functions in the legislative, administrative, and consensual processes of making law to meet the demands of the environment are of great importance. I defer their consideration until his functions in the making and administration of law through the courts are considered at some length.

This source of law is not generally understood by laymen and is not approved by all lawyers. Though the creation of the ages, it is often condemned as judge-made-law or judicial legislation. Whatever the source of law—constitution—statute—administrative practice—private document—or common law principle, its scope and significant application will sooner or later be involved in some controversy brought to the courts for determination. In this broad sense all law is the product of the litigation process, and since the litigation process itself is an important environmental factor, the law, as determined through it, not infrequently has considerable influence on the development of the environment.

When courts became established as essential to the functioning of government, lawyers—and a process by which people could seek the protection of their rights through the courts—became a necessity. The process is not simple and is not widely understood. It is ponderous, complex, costly, time-consuming, and uncertain in outcome. But in these seeming evils may be found many virtues—virtues that can never be surrendered to the computer. The litigants provide the controversy, and together with prospective witnesses and their data supply the details of fact from which the lawyers develop theories of liability and defense, supported by proof when the case comes to trial before a judge, with or without a jury. The issues of fact developed in the trial are submitted under the instructions of law given by the judge, and on the basis of the findings by judge or jury, judgment is rendered. If dissatisfied with the judgment, a litigant may seek a new trial and if this is denied may seek a reversal of the judgment by an appellate court on the basis of errors made in the trial court. After hearing, the appellate court will render its judgment usually supported by an opinion indicating the law which controls the court's judgment.

This is an oversimplification of the process and in no manner reflects the important roles played by the litigants, witnesses, jurors, trial and appellate judges, the lawyers, and the particular environment in which the case is adjudicated. The process is primarily under the direction of the lawyers with supervision by the judges. The raw materials of law and fact and the issues in the first instance are given form and expression by the artistry, or the lack of it, of the lawyers. The end product (the decision and the supporting opinion) is that of the court of final jurisdiction, greatly influenced if not determined by the creative work of the lawyers and the others who man the litigation production line. I would nowise discount the functions of judges, but it is through the *process* that law is made and not alone by those who refine, grade, and tag the finished product.

The final judgment settles the dispute of the parties and creates a precedent that may influence the decisions of future cases. The doctrine of precedent is the most important doctrine of the common law. It was developed to serve uniform administration throughout a judicial system of many courts and thus stabilize the law in the particular jurisdiction, and it serves this purpose well.

The greatest value of precedent, however, is its creative function. It usually provides a choice of law and frees a court to do what should be done and at the same time provides an impregnable basis for doing it—a very useful device in the hands of able advocates and able judges for making law responsive to the demands of the environment. Every decision of a court of final jurisdiction is a precedent for something. But for what? A decision based on particular facts not infrequently has different meanings for different lawyers and judges, for language is unstable and a decision may be held a precedent for different and even inconsistent judgments. In other words, lawyers and judges create out of former decisions the precedents they desire to follow. Even the language of Holy Writ has this infirmity and this strength and flexibility. Judges are fully aware of the creative power of their decisions and are greatly concerned—sometimes unduly so—as to their effect on future cases. This leads to much "over-speaking" of what they do. They seek to nail down the law with words as though what they do and say in one case is to endure forever as the basis for decision in cases yet to arise, and then spend years construing, qualifying, avoiding, or even rejecting what they have said and done, seemingly oblivious to the fact that whatever they continue to say and do make more precedents. Out of the materials of a multitude of precedents and much "over-speaking," advocates and judges find precedents for supporting any decision they think is just.

IV

There is no other area of law in which the courts of common law jurisdiction have so freely made and remade law and precedents and have so drastically changed course in response to the environment, as in the law of torts. A brief recital of its development serves my purpose here. The law of libel, for example, designed to suppress a free press has become its chief support. The law of deceit that once gave the widest latitude to the trader's guile now gives his victim the strictest protection. The trespass and nuisance actions have recently been broadened by highly flexible legal and equitable remedies to meet the many dangers to land occupiers created by modern industrial operations. The immunities recognized for centuries of the members of the family against liability for injuries inflicted on other members have within the last decade been widely rejected. Likewise, the immunities of police officials for injuries inflicted on prisoners and the liability of doctors and other professional people for malpractice have, in recent years, become a major area of tort litigations. And the protection given traders and the creative artists of all types for their trade values is steadily increasing.

Perhaps the most dramatic responses over the widest area of tort law are found in the creation of the law of negligence to supplant the strict moral liability of medieval tort law. Until near the beginning of the 1800's, if one person hurt another, whether innocently or intentionally, he had to compensate the victim for his injuries. About that time the courts began a transformation of the *action of trespass-on-the-case-for-negligence* into the *action for negligence* under which they created so many defenses that by the middle of the 1800's it was almost impossible to impose liability for personal injury, and there was no remedy at all for wrongful death.

The 1800's were a century of unprecedented industrial expansion, trade and commerce based on extensive construction, and operation of factories, railways, highways, canals, shipbuilding, docks, warehouses, merchandise marts, and supporting enterprises, all largely dependent in some degree upon the invention of numerous power driven machines, new tools, and processes. Adults and children were employed in great numbers, and many were injured and killed as a result of the imperfections of the machines and tools, their own ineptness or lack of training and that of their fellow employees, the risks that arose from unsafe places to work, and the inadequate organization and regulations under which they worked.

It may seem strange that instead of requiring protection and providing remedies for the victims of these dangerous group enterprises, the courts created numerous defenses that almost completely immunized those enterprises from any liability for the injuries resulting from negligent operations, defective products, dangerous premises, or otherwise. Landowners, municipalities, charitable institutions, and users of the highways shared similar immunities.

The specific defenses were numerous and were rapidly created.

The courts had no doubts about their power and function to discard old law and create new law. Their timidity came later probably as a result of the attacks on the courts by Jeremy Bentham and by early legislatures in this country.

There were many reasons why the courts approached the zero limits of liability imposed on enterprise through the use of these new defenses. Aside from the fact that the judges were cautious about sharing power with juries, the reasons for cutting liability short boiled down, *first*, to protect the courts against a flood of litigation beyond their capacity to administer; and *second*, to protect the infant industries so essential to trade, commerce, economic progress, and financial stability. These themes were worked over and enlarged upon in the leading cases of the period.

It is noteworthy that these defenses were first modified in cases involving railroads. In the middle of the nineteenth century, Lord Campbell's wrongful death act, at first designed to meet the rising toll of deaths from the early railroad operations, was broadened and enacted to cover all death cases. The act was greatly weakened by the courts imposing on it all the defenses they had created to limit liability for personal injuries. But it served to slow the headlong retreat from the strict liability imposed by medieval law and was the pattern for most of the death acts of the American states. In the railroad cases that followed in the last half of the 1800's, the change in the attitude of the courts served to modify practically all the defenses in all negligence cases and to develop an important group of doctrines that still serve to lighten the burdens required to sustain a victim's cause of action.

Why were the railroads the first to feel the reaction against the early negligence defenses? They were the first great enterprise group to extend their operations throughout the country and by all odds the most sought after and most highly rated industry a community could attract. But they kicked their friends in the teeth. They made enemies of the farmers and other landowners by their ruthless methods of construction; they created fire hazards for homes, businesses, crops, forests, and pastures; they ran down people and livestock caught on their tracks; they made the highways unsafe for horse and buggy traffic and killed people at highway crossings; their operations were dangerous for their workmen, and their wrecks killed and injured passengers. They were thought to be rich and powerful; their promoters unscrupulously bribed legislators, issued watered stock, and pocketed the proceeds. They granted rebates to the powerful and overcharged the weak. Their officials were vulgar in the display of their wealth and power; their public relations callous. They refused to pay for the injuries they caused until they were hauled into court. As might be expected they found the local courthouse hostile. Their able and well paid lawyers with their lengthy records of errors were called upon to rescue the cases they lost in the trial courts by their superior talents as advocates in the appellate courts, and for awhile they were successful .in prevailing upon the courts in further complicating the doctrines of negligence law. But more and more these doctrines were blunted, and many trial errors became harmless.

For the past forty years the courts have spent much of their time further modifying or altogether rejecting most of the negligence defenses of the 1800's. So today, though the negligence landscape is spotty, it can be said that employers (in cases that do not fall within workmen's compensation), landowners, manufacturers, processors, dealers, builders, contractors, and charitable and other service institutions have lost most of their immunities and are subject to the general negligence formula that is becoming increasingly exacting. Indeed, most of these defendants have been brought under strict liability for injuries resulting from their defective products and faulty services. Many important jurisdictions either by statute or court decision have stripped the government and its agencies of their immunities, and other courts, weary of waiting on legislative action, are threatening to do their own house-cleaning unless the legislatures do so promptly.

Why such wide rejection and reconditioning of early negligence law in the current century? Among the more important environmental influences are these.

The dangers created by the machines, operations, processes, and products of large enterprise have multiplied many times and so have their victims. Enterprise imposes its dangers on densely populated areas, creates the risks, enjoys the profits, can best provide protection against the dangers, and is able to share the losses as part of its business expense. The individual and small enterprise that create dangers have available insurance at relatively low costs provided by great business institutions for the purpose of protecting their customers from losses due to liabilities incurred under law.

Also, medical and other sciences now permit proof with considerable accuracy of the seriousness of injuries suffered by victims. For example, not very long ago emotional injury was dismissed with a sneer. No intelligent person sneers any more. Human life without emotions is without value and is of little value in absence of healthy emotions. The human being is a unity; the body and its marvelous structure serve primarily to develop, store, and transmit emotional power. This realization came to the courts only in this century and gave law's protection of the person its greatest expansion. What science has done in this respect has been repeated in some degree in all other cases of serious losses that come to the courts. Experts are available for making proof in all areas of law, and the lawyer who goes to the courthouse must be able to talk on equal terms the language of his own experts and of the experts of his opponent if he is to register in the minds of judges and jurors the injuries his client has suffered. While in no single jurisdiction has all the rubbish of nineteenth century negligence law been removed and replaced by doctrines and procedures that respond to the twentieth century environment, the movement is far advanced in all jurisdictions. Moreover, there is reason to believe that similar responses have been and are being made in the other areas of the common law. Those more competent to make this judgment have so indicated.

V

With the lawmaking power of the litigation process to the lawyer's credit, I now turn to the combined legislative, administrative, consensual, and litigation processes in their efforts to meet the problems created by the powerful groups of the social order.

In the early 1900's many of these groups had become so entrenched in their control of certain segments of our state and federal governments that it was thought impossible to break their hold. Some progress had been made, at least on paper, by creating the Interstate Commerce Commission, the Sherman Antitrust Act, the Clayton Act, and later the Federal Trade Commission. The implementation of each was retarded by World War I. Then followed the economic catastrophe of the thirties. I suppose the response of Congress and the state legislatures to the great Depression and later to the problems of World War II are the most dramatic instances of the lawyers' services of our day— mostly the services of young, courageous, and resourceful lawyers. Here it was necessary to create numerous commissions, bureaus, boards, and agencies to whom authority was delegated to make and administer law on many fronts far beyond the reach of the orthodox executive, legislative, and judicial departments of government.

In a very short period came the Securities and Exchange Commission—the National Labor Relations Board—expansion of the Agricultural, Commerce, and Interior Departments—a strong Antitrust Division of the Department of Justice—the Federal Aviation Authority and the Civil Aeronautics Board—the Wage and Hours Administration—the Food and Drug Division—Price Control—the Federal Communications Commission—the Tennessee Valley Authority—an expanded Federal Power Commission—the Internal Revenue Service—and numerous other important divisions and agencies—a veritable avalanche of new lawmaking and law administration bodies concerned with group power and its abuses, with only the supervisory power of the courts to keep them in bounds. Numerous additional agencies, reorganizations, and expansions have followed to meet specific group problems, and adjustments to the basic structures of the national government still are being made. In a much less degree, there have been similar developments in the states.

No one who did not witness the severe trauma suffered by the older lawyers, including many judges and scholars of that period, can believe their violent reactions to these remedial measures. Their unrelenting opposition created the necessity of unpacking the Supreme Court itself of its solid majority of judges who, heedless of the demands of the social and economic environments, for some years blocked all efforts of Congress, state legislatures, the executive, and the administration of the agencies to meet the abuses of group power that had become so flagrant. Here through thousands of officials with slight experience and few precedents to follow, a great mass of working procedures and everyday law was made and administered. If approved, the process was called administrative regulation; if disapproved, it was called arbitrary bureaucratic stupidity.

Perhaps of equal importance with the administrative bureaucracy, but not generally so recognized, is the making and expansion of law through daily transactions of people who render services and engage in trade and other affairs. These transactions and their variations in material details are infinite. Thousands of lawyers are engaged in reducing them to formal documents: conveyances of land, wills, trusts, contracts of employment, sales of goods, construction contracts, organizations of corporate and other institutions, and all the other consensual dealings involved in the affairs of millions of people. These documents are prepared with an eye on both statutes and court decisions in the hope that if subjected to litigation they will withstand attack and protect the interests of the parties as designed. Many provisions of these documents may go far beyond the perimeter of statute or decision, but as between the parties they serve the purposes of law and, if litigated, are the raw materials out of which law is made to influence innumerable transactions to come. They represent the lawyer's thrust to meet the environmental demands of those who operate in the feverish world of business affairs. Many of them serve to expand the power of the already powerful groups of our society.

Some of the statutes enacted by legislatures, some of the findings and orders of the numerous administrative agencies, and some of the contracts and other transactions formulated and executed under the directions of practicing lawyers are not designed to serve the public interest or to restrain the abuse of power by the groups that so largely dominate the affairs of our social order. The abuses of group power still remain and seemingly increase as rapidly as new controls are developed and even more rapidly if the legislative process or the regulating agency is itself made captive by the group it is designed to regulate. Some of our foremost citizens and officials believe the development of administrative controls that promised so much has proved a failure that only accentuates the abuse of power by dominant groups.

No one would claim that the excesses of group power have been curbed. Some groups find ways to escape their just burdens of taxation; market products known to be dangerous to the lives of consumers; amass great fortunes through excessive charges for insurance, money, and credit services; subsidize the channels of communication to inflame the prejudices, passions, and hates of those who are ignorant of their obligations to a free society; divert to their own pockets funds provided by taxation to relieve the sufferings of the weak and unfortunate; stall the enacting of remedies for great evils from which they profit; pervert the highest gifts with which human beings are endowed —the power to reproduce their kind and the power to express creative and ennobling ideas—to the vilest and most vulgar forms of indulgence and expression they can devise; deny their fellow citizens the basic rights of citizenship; undermine the high court that protects their rights and would blow our courthouses to fragments rather than submit their grievances to the orderly processes of law.

I wonder if we must await some destructive debacle to bring us to our senses—to make us happy to unite as one people—willing for the melting pot to do its work—freed from ancestral bondage of tragic histories in which none of us had a part or should want a part—one people who accept each other without reservation—a society to which all individuals and all groups give allegiance—where authority and loyalty, conformity and freedom are not in conflict. This problem of oneness is not of short duration. The more citizens who fail to understand its implications and the part they must play in its support, the more urgent oneness becomes and the more irresponsible those left outside.

There is much cleansing of mind and conscience to be done in the years ahead. Power alone will not sustain a social order dying of internal rot; neither will affluence. Nor does their combination insure social health. Despite the fact that many fortunes have been built and many people have prospered from the cumulative negative values of ignorance, waste, greed, fraud, vice, exploitation, and oppression, we cannot accept the philosophy that they serve the welfare of the social order. If these are the products of a group society their price comes too high even though much of the wealth so accumulated may eventually be turned to charity, religion, payment of taxes, education, and other good purposes.

VI

What is the response of law to an environment that nourishes such evils?

Lawyers write the laws, interpret the laws, administer the laws, represent the people who rely on the protection of the laws, man the courts in which the rights of people are litigated, and teach those who perform all these functions. No other group is entrusted with so much power over so broad a field of human affairs. Yet as a group it cannot exert its power to any great degree even in behalf of its own interests. Its impotency is endemic. Its members cannot cohere; they are individuals who spend most of their time thinking of the troubles of other people and give slight attention to their own affairs. In fact the great powers placed in the hands of lawyers are not for their own aggrandizement, but are the powers of the social order held in trust by lawyers for the protection of any person or any group whose interests are placed in jeopardy by others, even by the social order itself. For the most part, lawyers do their work individually and are always pitted against other lawyers either actually or prospectively. They cannot serve conflicting interests, and most of the interests they serve are in conflict with other interests that other lawyers serve. They find it difficult to agree on the solution of specific issues and have the same trouble that religionists and philosophers have in agreeing on doctrinal abstractions. Indeed, lawyers are trained to challenge, criticize, champion, argue, and disagree even concerning the interests of the government they serve, and at the same time they are trained to support by their advice and advocacy the rights of others under the law they challenge. Usually under the layman's question mark, trusted of necessity by his client, in the eyes of opposing client a bigger scoundrel than the client he serves, the lawyer's most reliable friend is himself—a friend he must never let down.

Yet these jousting knights of justice—bred to controversy, quick to attack or defend, and licensed to bring to bear the power of the social order itself to the adjustment of the affairs of their fellow beings —have developed remedies against many of the evils of the past and are now engaged in developing remedies to meet the evils arising out of the environments of today and tomorrow—remedies directed primarily at the abuses of group power. The agencies through which these remedies are sought are old in concept but must constantly undergo remodeling to enlarge their powers, clarify their procedures, and improve their administration.

If their great record of lawmaking and administration is as significant as I think it is, may I ask what the profession and the institutions through which it works must further do to meet the abuses of group power? This is no idle question—the stakes are high—the confrontation is no small or short engagement. It is found in every community—not limited to the campuses. The issues and the stakes are not clear to many of the participants, and many are fighting against their own interests and against their friends. Guerrilla social warfare on many levels in this country was never more intense, more brutal, or more senseless, and threatens to become more so.

When formal law is involved, legislatures, administrators, and lawyers who serve the people in their daily affairs must bear the brunt of battle. But it should now be clear in the current period of difficult social readjustment that the struggle for justice and stability has shifted beyond the effective reach of formal law, at least until the issues are more clearly drawn. Groups of many blends who have legitimate grievances and aspirations know little of formal law and even less of the irresistible compulsion of peaceful negotiation and compromise. They know how to demand, march, protest, demonstrate, harass, make fiery speeches, lash themselves into furies, threaten, engage in violence, terrorize, and infuriate their communities. Sometimes it seems their strategy is not to win but to lose at any price, and by their loss justify the destruction they seek. In the end they get the clubs of the police, the penalties of the courts, and the contempt of those who have given great support to their efforts to share the advantages and responsibilities of the social order.

These people are in need of counsel and need to be shown how to achieve their legitimate ends, if that is what they seek, through the clear formulation and decent presentation of their grievances and aspirations. Under the pressures of facts and good sense there is not the slightest doubt that they can gain full participation in the affairs of establishments they seek to displace—establishments that have brought them more recognition than has ever been achieved by any other people anywhere at any time. The establishments were never more inclined to accord to all citizens the responsibilities they can perform. Moreover, in their efforts to gain full acceptance by the social order, they can have the services and support of organizations of great influence in the community, and I know of no greater service the lawyer as a citizen can render than to make himself available to these organizations. In this direction he will find a new and vast dimension for his talents.

Should the efforts of negotiation fail, formal law is still in reserve for restraints and protection. The processes of the courts are open wide for the raw materials of controversy to clarify the issues and determine them under law. To some this process seems too slow and cautious. In fact, only a few decisions are required to accelerate social progress to match the speed of the environment, so vividly demonstrated by recent decisions of the Supreme Court that have blasted away obstructions that had denied millions of young people access to our schools and universities, denied citizens the values of their votes, and denied a fair trial to persons accused of crime—obstructions created and supported by strong political and other groups over a period of a century and more. *These, and numerous other decisions in their support, were the creative products of lawyers.* No lawyer who can assemble and present the data in support of his client's grievance need hesitate to seek the aid of the courts. When courts move courageously to determine the issues presented to them, they can remove many obstacles that block the way, and this is especially true when they utilize the preventive remedies at their command. *In a free society they have and must always have the power equal to any emergency of abuse of power.*

Of great importance in this never-ending procession of the social order is the educational improvement of its legal environment. As advocates and judges from modern law schools take the places of their predecessors, the metaphysical doctrines and obsolescent procedures of earlier periods play less and less part in all law. There is no moratorium in the reconditioning of old and the creation of new remedies. This has been recently demonstrated by the resurrection of the civil rights statutes of the 1860's and 1870's that lay dormant for so many years. There is scarcely a problem created by the inventions, scientific discoveries, business practices, and social disorders of this period that has not excited study by legal scholars, institutes of legal education, or some bar association committee. The profession and its members as a whole have never been so stirring in their work, so tireless in probing the problems emerging from the racing environment, and so energetic in speaking their minds through so many publications. Also, I may add that the courts have never been more receptive to fresh thought or more ready to find and extend the remedies at their command to check the abuses of power.

The Role of the Lawyer in America's Ghetto Society

NORMAN DORSEN

During a time of social unrest and violence, of sharp polarization of constituent groups within our varied culture, and of searching, cynical, and unfriendly criticism of public institutions—including law and legal institutions—will American lawyers play a constructive role in trying to solve the great problems that beset us, or will they perhaps add to them? This, in its most abstract form, is the question I shall discuss today.

Some of you may recall that when President Franklin Roosevelt spoke to the delegates to a national convention of the Daughters of the American Revolution he addressed them as "fellow immigrants." This salutation, I need hardly say, did not charm his audience. I hope that

NORMAN DORSEN, professor of law and director of the Arthur Garfield Hays Civil Liberties Program, New York University School of Law. Norman Dorsen received the B.A. degree from Columbia University (1950) and the LL.B. from Harvard University (1953). During the period 1953–1955, he was assistant to general counsel, Secretary of the Army; during 1956–1957 he was law clerk to Chief Judge Calvert Magruder, and law clerk to Justice John M. Harlan during 1957–1958. He was associate professor of law at New York University, 1961–1965, and has been professor since 1965. In 1968 he was visiting professor of law at the London School of Economics. His publications include *Frontiers of Civil Liberties* (1968), *Political and Civil Rights in the United States* (with Emerson and Haber, 1967), and *The Rights of Americans: What They Are, What They Should Be* (ed., 1971). He is general counsel of the American Civil Liberties Union; executive director of the Special Committee on Courtroom Conduct, Association of the Bar of the City of New York; and a member of the board of directors of the Association for the Study of Abortion. He also acted as consultant to the United States Violence Commission in 1968 and is consultant to Random House and National Educational Television.

I am running less risk when I salute the attorneys and law students here as "fellow ghetto lawyers."

Bear in mind that for the President to remind the ladies of the DAR that their ancestors did not walk across the water was not an insult. Similarly, my purpose in suggesting that we are all ghetto lawyers is merely to state the simple but important fact that most lawyers, now and throughout our history, have employed their professional skills to support particular segments of the population—generally the well-to-do classes. The rich also live in ghettos, and while these may be gilded, they effectively isolate their residents from the lives and travails of less fortunate groups.

Of course lawyers have not always served primarily the rich. This was true, for example, on the early American frontier, when lawyers adapted both their conduct and their practices to rough conditions. It is reliably reported that "some lawyers and judges displayed meanness in conduct and slovenliness in dress" with the purpose of appearing "democratic."[1] Pioneers were apparently "more apt to distrust and condemn a man for being 'kid-gloved' and 'silk-stockinged' than for lack of a clean shirt, drunkenness, or outright rudeness."[2] And in 1876 in New York City a legal aid office was opened for the first time. Although that office was designed to provide legal assistance to the poor, it is revealing to note—in view of my topic today—that it was financed by the German Society of New York, and only persons of German birth or origin were eligible for assistance.[3]

This pattern of exclusiveness has persisted. Scholarly studies of lawyers who handle most of the large commercial business in the country indicate that there are significant similarities between the clients and the lawyers who serve them. In the early 1960's more than seventy percent of Wall Street lawyers were graduates of the Harvard, Yale, or Columbia law schools, and thirty percent were listed in the Social Register.[4] These firms expressed a preference for lawyers "who are Nordic, have pleasing personalities and 'clean-cut' appearances, are graduates of the 'right' schools, have the 'right' social background and experience in the affairs of the world, and are endowed with tremendous stamina."[5] A Detroit study compared individual practitioners with lawyers in medium and large firms. It was found that the indi-

---

[1] 2 A. CHROUST, THE RISE OF THE LEGAL PROFESSION IN AMERICA 94-95 (1965).
[2] Id.
[3] E. BROWNELL, LEGAL AID IN THE UNITED STATES 7 (1951).
[4] E. SMIGEL, THE WALL STREET LAWYER 39 (1964).
[5] Id. at 37.

vidual practitioner was much more likely to have had a father who was manually employed, who was an entrepreneur, and whose family was originally from Eastern or Southern Europe. Moreover, fifty-nine percent of the individual practitioners were immigrants or the sons of immigrants whereas only ten percent of the firm members were. The individual practitioners tended to be Catholic or Jewish, while a high percentage of firm members were Protestant. Finally, the firms tended to do business and corporate work while the individual practitioners did what is often characterized as "dirty work"—personal injury, divorce, and criminal law.[6]

Neither of these studies—or similar ones that could be noted—is startling in result. They simply mirror the social pecking order and the fact that the ingredients of the American melting pot dissolve very slowly. They reflect, in short, the continued existence of a ghetto society and a ghettoized practice of law.

Considerable attention has been paid to these longstanding barriers within the legal profession, so I shall not dwell on them. Indeed, there is evidence that the pace of change has been quickening. Racial and religious bars to employment and advancement are coming down at a pretty fair rate, and women are beginning to assert the right to be treated on their merits. It is, therefore, ironic that a new division is rapidly developing in the legal profession—a division that reflects the political and social currents in the society at large. Lawyers divide among those who engage in public service law and those who do not. "Public service lawyers" may be found in every part of the profession and do not embody any particular political philosophy. They include all lawyers working to further the broadly based efforts to assist previously unrepresented interests in society by providing counsel to the poor, harmonizing relations between the races, assisting the consumer, protecting the environment, advancing individual rights, or otherwise acting for a public rather than a private purpose. There can be legitimate dispute over both ends and means in achieving these broad goals. The key question is whether the profession will adequately respond to interests that have not been able to attract legal resources in the marketplace.

For our purposes the practicing bar can be viewed in two broad categories. First are the "straight" lawyers, who are engaged in the traditional commercial practice of law, whether in large or small firms,

---

6 Ladinsky, *The Impact of Social Backgrounds of Lawyers on Law Practice and the Law*, 16 J. LEGAL ED. 127, 130-31, 139 (1963).

as sole practitioners, or in law departments of corporations. The second category consists of fulltime public service lawyers. Although it includes legal aid attorneys, lawyers in government service, and perhaps teachers of law, today I shall be discussing four other sorts of public service lawyers: civil liberties lawyers, poverty lawyers, the new breed of "radical" lawyers, and the practitioners in recently established public interest law firms. These four groups are composed principally of young activists motivated less by economic considerations than by the public purposes I have referred to. They are sometimes viewed as humanitarians and samaritans, sometimes as agitators and troublemakers. But whatever they are called, they are surely a class different from the small-town practitioner with middle-class clients or the Wall Street lawyer —in New York, Cleveland, or Dallas—who services mammoth corporations.

Let us first consider the traditional lawyer. Most of them are engaged in legal work that is strictly private; they concentrate on their clients' problems and live their own lives. This may include some community participation—service on a school or hospital board or as a church warden—that is unrelated to law practice (except as it may incidentally attract new business). Some of these lawyers aspire to public or judicial office, and others are content where they are. In any case the strictly private practitioner is not doing good enough, or doing enough good, for the ghetto society at this juncture in our history.

If this conclusion is not obvious, at least it has a proud lineage. Justice Harlan Fiske Stone speaking more than thirty-five years ago said,

> [I]n the new order which has been forced upon us, we cannot expect the Bar to function as it did in other days and under other conditions. . . . [T]here must be appraisal and comprehension of the new conditions and the changed relationships of the lawyer to his clients, to his professional brethren and to the public. That appraisal must pass beyond the petty details of form and manners which have been so largely the subject of our codes of ethics, to more fundamental consideration of the way in which our professional activities affect the welfare of society as a whole.[7]

What was true in 1934 remains true today, and indeed from the standpoint of the ghetto society—despondently similar in its social mani-

---

[7] Stone, *The Public Influence of the Bar*, 48 Harv. L. Rev. 1, 10 (1934).

festations to the depression society of the 1930's—Justice Stone's words have an intrusively contemporary quality.

Fortunately, many are responding to the challenge articulated by Justice Stone. Some are doing so in time-honored ways by accepting assignment to criminal cases without fee, representing politically unpopular individuals or groups, and providing free advice to public institutions. But this is not all. There is a new and spreading commitment by law firms in all parts of the country to broader public service *on firm time and with firm resources.* This commitment has been spurred by student interest and demands and has reflected the fact, stated in a memorandum prepared by a large New York firm, that lawyers "have undoubtedly become more aware in recent years of this country's social problems and their relationships to professional responsibility."[8] The point is made even more sharply by a Washington firm that has said, "If there is one lesson to be drawn from events on campuses and in the ghettos, it is that persons, institutions, organizations, and firms cannot simply pursue their parochial interest in disregard of the demands of our time. . . ."[9]

Consistent with these general statements many large law firms in Cleveland, Baltimore, Los Angeles, and elsewhere, as well as in New York and Washington, recently have institutionalized their public service efforts and are engaging in wide-ranging active efforts that have come to be known as *pro bono* work.[10] Thus established firms (1) have represented individuals challenging racial segregation in North and South, citizens engaging in rent strikes, and Indians, Mexican-Americans, and other minorities attempting to assert legal rights; (2) have financed branch offices in ghetto areas to provide free legal services to the poor, and have placed associates in existing neighborhood legal services offices for the same purpose; (3) have provided free counsel to private bodies imbued with a public purpose such as the American Civil Liberties Union, educational television stations, and ghetto organizations like the Bedford-Stuyvesant Development Corporation; (4) have established public interest branches or assigned partners and associates to work exclusively on civil rights, welfare, consumer, and similar matters, usually of their own choosing.

This catalogue, which could be considerably expanded,[11] surely

---

8 Memorandum dated Oct. 3, 1969, on file in New York University School of Law Placement Office.

9 Berman & Cahn, *Bargaining for Justice: The Law Students' Challenge to Law Firms,* 5 HARV. CIV. RIGHTS–CIV. LIB. L. REV. 16, 23 (1970).

10 *Id.* at 24-25.

11 One example of an important legal victory won by a major law firm acting in

represents a major step forward from conditions of only a few years ago. Nevertheless, judging from the questions that are being asked about big firm public service law, these impressive gains may be merely harbingers of things to come. In the first place, only a minority of firms engage in *pro bono* work. Secondly, when a firm says that it "encourages" such work, it is often not clear whether this merely means its lawyers may work on their own time—that is, when it does not interfere with fee-generating business. Thirdly, it is still too early to tell, at least in many firms, whether associates (or even partners) who tend to concentrate on *pro bono* work are taking risks with their careers.

Critics of the status quo are not content with asking questions. A systematic strategy has now been proposed to bring pressure on law firms and focus attention on the problem of law firm public interest work. Two public interest lawyers have suggested, among other tactics, that law students use questionnaires to obtain detailed data on the *pro bono* activities of law firms, that placement offices require firms to reveal such data as a condition of interviewing at the school, that the information be made public by a national "reporter" system, and that students be encouraged to bargain collectively with law firms— not to secure private benefits for themselves but to encourage law firm reform.[12]

One can easily visualize the ire of most lawyers in the face of this aggressive strategy. Even those who are sympathetic to public service lawyering may have reservations about some of the tactics outlined above, reflecting I suppose both a concern for the privacy and autonomy of private practitioners as well as a lingering nostalgia for quieter times.

But these doubts may reflect a premise that is increasingly under attack: that law firms are private rather than public institutions. Many law students and young lawyers would dispute this assumption, not from a narrow or technically legal standpoint, but in practical recognition of the impact of these institutions on American society. Just as many private universities have acknowledged that they perform a public

---

[11] One example of an important legal victory won by a major law firm acting in the public interest is Moss v. CAB, No. 23,627 (D.C. Cir., July 9, 1970). The court invalidated a Board order approving higher fares for passengers. Stanford Ross, Esq., and his colleagues, acting for a group of congressmen challenging the higher rates, served without fee in a complex law suit. *See generally* 79 YALE L.J. 1005-1198 (1970), which appeared after this Article went to press.

[12] Berman & Cahn, *supra* note 9, at 26-30.

function with important responsibilities to the community at large, so too perhaps should firms of lawyers engaged in a practice that is national in scope, services the country's largest industries, generates millions of dollars in fees, and touches on the public interest at countless points.

Whether or not one accepts the broad sweep of these assertions, it is well to recall that many large firms have already completed student and placement office questionnaires that reveal information concerning firm hiring policy, *pro bono* work, potential conflicts of interest, and political and charitable activities of individual lawyers. In the face of this willingness to disclose, it is difficult to view the firm as the private enclave it once was thought to be.

The issue has been carried still further, most notably by Ralph Nader and his associates. They have questioned the propriety of lawyers' advocating positions on behalf of clients contrary to the public interest, particularly in the area of public health and safety. Mr. Nader recently criticized lawyers for "hiding behind their responsibility to those clients, and not taking the burden of their advocacy as the canons of ethics advised them to do wherever the public interest is importantly involved."[13] Following this line, one of Mr. Nader's associates has recently suggested that it is a betrayal of the public interest for a lawyer to exhaust every possible administrative and legal remedy to keep a dangerous drug on the market an extra year, to lobby extensively to modify or remove a label warning on a drug, or to weaken the provisions of a traffic safety act in the economic interests of the automotive industry. These are serious charges. If accepted they would undermine the undivided loyalty that attorneys traditionally have bestowed on their clients, because lawyers would have an independent obligation to consider the "public interest" in the course of giving advice or representing their clients.

It seems to me that two distinct questions are presented. The first is whether lawyers should decline to represent potential clients whose goals are thought to be improper. The second is whether, once a client is accepted, lawyers should temper their efforts by taking into account their view of the public interest.

On the first question my opinion is pretty clear. I do not think we should breach in the slightest the long and healthy tradition that permits and indeed encourages lawyers to represent all sorts of de-

---

13 Nader, *Law Schools and Law Firms*, THE NEW REPUBLIC, Oct. 11, 1969, at 23. *See also* Green, *Law Graduates: The New Breed*, THE NATION, June 1, 1970, at 658.

spised groups and individuals, including rapists, gangsters, and Communists. Once it is decided that it violates the common good to represent a particular drug, auto, or tobacco company, before very long the arbiters of public interest—that is, everyone—will determine that radicals, homosexuals, and segregationists are not entitled to counsel. This is not a pleasant prospect for me to contemplate—and not only because, under the auspices of the American Civil Liberties Union, I have personally represented radicals, homosexuals, and segregationists. To permit lawyers to turn away clients because of the "public interest" would, in my judgment, be inconsistent with the public interest in assuring representation for weak and despised groups in society.

My conclusion on the first question presented by Mr. Nader is matched by my certitude that the issue is largely academic. In the commercial setting clients do not go begging for long, and there is no reason to assume that the current debate will lead to a speedy change in the economic facts of life. In other words, there is no real chance that "unpopular" corporate defendants will lack lawyers willing to serve them.

The second question Mr. Nader raises is far more difficult. He suggests there are limits imposed on the lawyer's advocacy by the demands of the "public interest," notwithstanding the traditional lawyer-client relationship. This has led to some pretty sharp comment. Because of his attacks on lawyers who transgress his particular definition of the common good, Mr. Nader has even been likened to the late Senator Joe McCarthy. More temperate, but equally unfriendly, was a recent editorial in the American Bar Association Journal.[14] Reasons for rejecting Mr. Nader's approach were also elaborated in a memorandum prepared by a major Washington law firm:

> Before effective consumer or other legislation can be framed, many facts have to be developed and understood. Costs and benefits have to be measured. When a productive effort produces an evil side effect, measures must be carefully framed to root out the evil without injuring the productive process itself. Effective advocacy of opposing views serves to sharpen these issues, and to identify where the public interest really lies.[15]

Despite the chorus of criticism, I do not believe summary judgment against Mr. Nader is appropriate. In the first place, it should be recalled that already there are important limits, imposed by the Canons of Ethics, on the modes of advocacy permitted a lawyer. He may not lie,

---

[14] *Mr. Nader's Legal Profession*, 56 A.B.A.J. 146 (1970).
[15] Memorandum dated Dec. 1, 1969, on file in New York University School of Law Placement Office.

knowingly misquote a document or witness, refer in argument to a fact not yet proved, or file a pleading he knows to be factually unsupported.[16] Although these limitations all relate to the internal integrity of the judicial process, they that suggest lawyers are not free to disregard claims of fairness imposed by public policy. This, in turn, suggests there may be limits to the tactics of litigation or lobbying that can be employed on behalf of a client; there may be arguments so frivolous that to assert them is tantamount to delay and obstructiveness. The initial responsibility, of course, rest with courts and agencies to make it costly for lawyers to engage in these tactics, but surely some responsibility rests with the bar also. Thus Robert T. Swaine of Cravath, Swaine, and Moore once confessed, "Probably too frequently our advice has been too limited to technical validity of proposed action without regard to its social or economic implications."[17] And the very firm whose memorandum is quoted above has made this statement:

> We set what we believe to be rigorous ethical standards, and we adhere to them . . . . We do not always come out in full agreement with the policy views of our clients in every instance, any more than the views of all members of the firm accord with one another. But we do not make arguments or take positions which we believe to be outside the bounds of reasonable and responsible advocacy.[18]

Obviously, if an obligation to take positions only within the "bounds of reasonable and responsible advocacy" is recognized, important ground is conceded. Indeed, from this and other indications it appears the two sides in this dispute may be closer together than either acknowledges.

Those defending the traditional advocate's role of private practitioners point to the lack of a satisfactory definition of "public interest" to guide lawyers in representing clients, to the risk that a standard this vague is a many-edged sword that would cut in unexpected directions to impair the rights of varied unpopular clients, and to the complexity of the issues (once rhetoric is stripped away) relating to automobile safety, water and air pollution, and other "public interest" matters.[19] Not surprisingly, established private practitioners put forward these contentions with some fervor not only because they believe they have rendered valuable service over the years to their clients

---

16 ABA CANONS OF PROFESSIONAL ETHICS Nos. 15 & 22.

17 Swaine, *Impact of Big Business on the Profession: An Answer to Critics of the Modern Bar*, 35 A.B.A.J. 89, 170 (1949).

18 Memorandum, *supra* note 15.

19 *See* Cutler, Book Review, 83 HARV. L. REV. 1746, 1751-52 (1970).

—and that this itself is in the "public interest"—but because they feel threatened personally by the sharp criticisms now being made of their careers and lifework.

Notwithstanding their vehement defense, the most visible spokesmen for the established bar neither ignore the public interest nor embrace the half-joking dictum of Macauley, who said that we obtain the best decision "when two men argue, as unfairly as possible, on opposite sides."[20] If law firms would recognize the obligation to indulge only in "reasonable and responsible advocacy" a large area of disagreement would disappear.

But not all. The critics, led by Ralph Nader, very likely would insist that this obligation be generally acknowledged by the organized bar, that lawyers representing private interests face squarely the issue whether they are being asked to take irresponsible positions (for example, to delay intentionally the resolution of a controversy involving product safety or water pollution), and that, because of the lucrative attractions of private practice, lawyers should assume the burden of proof to justify proposed legal action that arguably is contrary to the public interest.

I think this approach is warranted. A lawyer asked to oppose automobile safety proposals, more onerous requirements for manufacturing near rivers and streams, or clearer labeling on consumer goods, must close his door and in his own conscience determine whether the positions he is being asked to take are ethically justifiable. To recommend this sort of soul-searching is not naïve. If firms and individuals would examine the implications of their professional roles and set limits on advocacy for private interests—as I understand at least one Washington firm has now agreed to do—the consequences are bound to be healthy.

A particular obligation should rest on lawyers engaged in lobbying before legislatures and administrative agencies. There is an important distinction between this type of law practice and judicial proceedings, as pointed out by Louis Brandeis in 1905 in terms that are still apt:

> In the first place, the counsel selected to represent important private interests possesses usually ability of a high order, while the public is often inadequately represented or wholly unrepresented. That presents a condition of great unfairness to the public. As a result many bills pass in our legislatures which would not have become law if the public interest had been fairly represented; and many good bills are defeated which if supported by able lawyers would have been enacted.

20 J. FRANK, COURTS ON TRIAL 80 (1949).

. . . Some men of high professional standing have even en-
deavored to justify their course in advocating professionally
legislation which in their character as citizens they would
have voted against.[21]

There can be dispute about whether the conduct condemned by
Justice Brandeis should be professionally banned. A leading Washington practitioner has suggested that what Brandeis "had in mind was
not a canon of ethics, but a personal standard by which we judge not
only the clients we are willing to represent, but also the extent to
which we will seek to include in our professional advice and assistance
a consideration of national affairs."[22] Whether or not this is what
Brandeis had in mind, it is unacceptable for lawyers "to ignore entirely
the larger interests of the country and the basic standards of decency
in the process of stringing together sets of legal loopholes to achieve
some inordinate advantage."[23] Unfortunately there is evidence that this
is what frequently occurs.[24]

I turn now to the second broad class of attorneys, fulltime public
service lawyers. I have said that I shall discuss four types of these
lawyers to illustrate the theme that the profession has opportunities
as well as difficult choices to make in the way it serves the public interest and the ghetto society. These four types are the practitioner in
the new public interest law firms, the so-called "radical lawyer," the
civil liberties lawyer, and the poverty lawyer.

Before discussing these types individually, I would like to draw
attention to an important indicia of the general attitude of these public
service lawyers—their approach to the lawyer's craft. The best statement I know of the craftsman's ideal is not by a lawyer but by the
novelist Joseph Conrad, who wrote as follows in *The Mirror of the
Sea*:

Now the moral side of an industry . . . is the attainment and
preservation of the highest possible skill on the part of the
craftsman. Such skill, the skill of technique, is more than
honesty; it is something wider, embracing honesty and grace

---

21 Brandeis, *The Opportunity in the Law*, 39 Am. L. Rev. 555, 561 (1905). Brandeis
was speaking before the days of wide congressional delegation to administrative bodies,
but there is little doubt he would have included practice before such agencies within
the scope of his comments. For more recent analysis, see Mikva, *Interest Representation
in Congress: The Social Responsibility of the Washington Lawyer*, 38 Geo. Wash. L. Rev.
651 (1970).
22 C. Horsky, The Washington Lawyer 140 (1952).
23 *Id.* at 140-41.
24 *See* Riley, *The Challenge of the New Lawyers: Public Interest and Private Clients*,
38 Geo. Wash. L. Rev. 547 (1970).

and rule in an elevated and clear sentiment . . . . It is made
up of accumulated tradition, kept alive by individual pride,
rendered exact by professional opinion, and, like the higher
arts, it is spurred on and sustained by discriminating praise.[25]

Not very long ago, when I was a student, the sense of the craft
ranked virtually supreme in the scale of values. It was extolled by
Holmes and Hand, and it had the virtue of reflecting the most neutral
of all principles—art for art's sake. But that was the rub. Just as an
earlier generation had questioned a positivistic view of the law that
tended to exclude moral values, the current generation has sensed and
rejected—properly in my view—an arid concentration on craft at the
expense of social concerns. Craft, after all, is a tool that can serve any
master.

The law schools, I am proud to say, have played an instrumental
role in altering the focus of young lawyers. Increasingly, the emphasis
there is on where we are going in the law and in society, and not only
on how to make the journey efficient and comfortable. This is not a
new development, but it has gained new momentum in recent years,
and the widening impact on students is plainly visible.

The greater danger now, it seems to me, is that students will
unduly depreciate the values extolled by Conrad and therefore reduce
their efforts to achieve the craftsman's perfection. This risk is especially
great among fulltime public service lawyers because they usually have
a heavy docket and limited resources and simply lack the time to
prepare a finished product. In addition, such lawyers, especially in
politically sensitive cases, sometimes fall prey to the dispiriting attitude
that the judge's philosophy will govern irrespective of the technical
competence of the lawyer and sometimes even to the conceit that the
political virtues of a case (as they view them) guarantee a favorable
result. My own experience is to the contrary. Rigorous attention to
detail and a willingness to work and rework one's efforts remain the
lawyer's indispensable allies; in short, I am confident that a noble
purpose will never be a substitute for Shepard's Citations.

Now let me consider the public service lawyers themselves. First,
a word on the public interest law firms that are beginning to mush-
room. One of these firms, the Center for Law and Social Policy in
Washington, has four lawyers and a distinguished board of trustees. It
already has a full docket of cases on juvenile problems, mental health,

---

[25] J. CONRAD, 4 COMPLETE WORKS 24 (1924).

the environment, and consumer protection, and it is forging strong links with universities and men in public office. This firm and others like it are, of course, the logical extension of the practitioner's desire to devote his energies to public questions and to do so unburdened by the demands of private practice, including the kinds of ethical questions that we have already discussed. To secure financing for such ventures is not easy, but as long as it can be obtained the returns for the public interest are bound to be substantial.

The second category of public service lawyer—the "radical"—is in many ways the most fascinating. The genre is exemplified if not typified by William Kunstler, attorney for the Chicago Seven. Many young lawyers and law students identify with Kunstler, Black Panther lawyer Gerald Lefcourt, and their colleagues. Lefcourt has said, "Youth—that's what it's all about. In three or four years we're going to turn the legal system upside down." Many radical lawyers give support to the idea of revolution although there is a certain fuzziness about what this means. But there is no ambiguity about their expressed commitment to destroy poverty, racism, and injustice, which they feel have become institutionalized in the American system. Accordingly, they see the necessity for revolutionary change in that system, and thus many of them are not seriously concerned with having better laws enacted, improving the legal system, or any other reforms that do not affect the underlying institutions. The radical lawyer views himself as little different from the writer, the truckdriver, the typist, and the arms expert—each possessing useful skills for revolutionary activity. He believes his main mission to be "keeping his friends on the street, where they can take care of business."[26] In addition, the radical lawyer is developing new sorts of relationships with clients resulting from their mutual understanding that the chief consideration in any lawsuit is not law but politics; the lawyer and his client must jointly determine "legal" tactics that best serve their political ends.[27]

Despite the rhetoric, there is something anomalous about the idea of a revolutionary lawyer. After all, lawyers by definition are trained to work within an ongoing legal order—to negotiate, to compromise, to settle. These activities are not compatible with violent revolution. It is no wonder, therefore, that many radical lawyers sound suspiciously like zealous reformers. Thus, Professor Richard Wasserstrom in a re-

---

[26] Memorandum to the author from a "radical lawyer," entitled "Poverty Lawyer as Radical," undated.
[27] *Id.*

cent speech on "Lawyers and Revolution" concluded that the job the radical lawyer is "singularly equipped to perform is that of being truly imaginative in consideration of the fundamental ways in which a legal system might be transformed and yet remain a system that does those things that ought to be done and that a legal system now does."[28] This formulation is entirely sensible, but it does not seem particularly daring.

Whichever version of the radical lawyer one adopts, no doubt most of our fellow citizens view him as a threat, or at least a pest, and certainly not as a "public interest lawyer." There are some, however, who may see him primarily as an outgrowth of unresolved ills in American society. After all, like it or not, the young people who rally to the radical flag are our progeny, born and reared here in the United States and not in an alien land. I shall say no more now about radical lawyers, but we certainly will be hearing more from them.

I turn now to the civil liberties lawyer. Although he has become a fixture on the legal landscape, he finds himself increasingly unsure these days about just what is a civil liberties issue. It used to be relatively easy; the contours of due process, equal protection, and the first amendment, while constantly changing, were familiar benchmarks to those seeking to protect individual rights. No longer. The American Civil Liberties Union has now determined that it violates civil liberties to impose capital punishment, to prohibit the use of marijuana by criminal sanctions, to deny the vote to eighteen-year-olds, to perpetuate the electoral college, and to conscript soldiers under the present draft law. The Union has also adopted policies in support of community control when this aids equal treatment, is debating whether to act in the field of environmental protection, and only recently defeated proposals to put the Union on record in favor of a guaranteed annual income.

Bearing in mind that the ACLU does not take positions on the general desirability of legislative proposals but only on whether a civil liberties issue is presented, how should these questions have been resolved? Even allowing for individual variations, two broad approaches can be discerned within the Union. One philosophy—regarded as "traditional"—relies heavily on familiar interpretations of the Bill of Rights, fearing that if the Union wanders afield it will be subject to the charge that it is merely another liberal political organization with no special warrant to be heard in constitutional controversies. This

---

[28] Wasserstrom, *Postscript: Lawyers and Revolution*, 30 U. Pitt. L. Rev. 125, 132 (1968).

view also emphasizes the importance of conserving organizational capital and not squandering it in disputes—for example, over the eighteen-year-old vote—in which the civil liberties component is secondary to other considerations. Finally, the traditional view sees the Union as a useful conduit between American dissenters and the Establishment, an important mediating influence that could quickly be jeopardized if the ACLU becomes identified with radical or political positions.

The competing ACLU philosophy is more activist. Its proponents point out that the Union has never been wedded to existing constitutional doctrine but has viewed itself as the responsible agent of the future in the Supreme Court and in the legislatures. In addition they maintain that the ACLU should not be concerned about the unpopularity or the political implications of its positions and should call the issues as they see them, however novel and controversial these may be. As for the merits themselves, the Union's activists argue that much doctrinal innovation can be justified by radiations of the single, seminal principle that whenever government acts to restrict individual liberty or to withhold important benefits available to others, a strong presumption exists that a civil liberties violation has occurred.

These conflicting contentions obviously cannot be resolved in the abstract but must be settled case by case. My own general preferences, therefore, may be more easily understood if I record my votes as a member of the Union's Board of Directors. While I had doubts about the application of the one man-one vote principle to the election of the President in a constitutionally ordained federal system, I eventually concluded that a civil liberties issue was in fact presented in that case and each of the others I have mentioned in which the Union has spoken, except the guaranteed annual income. In that instance, while I believe that the necessities of life are essential to an individual's ability to assert and enjoy conventional civil liberties, I nevertheless felt that the guaranteed income should not be designated a civil liberties issue. It seemed to me that because the ACLU lacked authority and expertness in the economic sphere and would have had no basis for specifying the reach of the new principle, a foray into economics would have left the Union open to the charge of political expediency, at cost to the public credibility of the organization and the principles that it has long championed.

The final prototype of the public service lawyer is the poverty lawyer. Ever since 1876, as we have already observed, attorneys have provided free legal services to the poor with the burden borne chiefly

by legal aid and defender offices. But until the establishment of the
Legal Services Program in the Office of Economic Opportunity in 1965,
there was no large-scale commitment to the ideal of a lawyer for everyone in need.

This new and ambitious program presented serious problems,
emanating chiefly from dollar limitations and local political opposition. The principal dilemma has been whether the poverty lawyer in
a Harlem storefront or rural Mississippi county should direct his main
efforts, and his inadequate resources, to providing more and better
representation for individuals or to achieving social, economic, and
legal reform through the litigation of test cases.[29] The advocates of both
positions articulate their views in terms of the needs and desires of
the poor community, but they also can be explained by the economic
and intellectual interests of the contending groups. Neither side, in my
judgment, has dominated the argument. The reformers have won some
great victories, affecting the lives of many poor people (such as the
residence and man-in-the-house welfare cases), but they frequently have
failed to represent the interests of individual clients by refusing "little"
cases so that they can work on "big" ones. On the other hand, those who
genuinely wish to serve individual clients are often subject to the influence of local political organizations and many times have proved
corrupt or professionally incompetent and sometimes both.

The bar associations probably have the ultimate power through
their contacts in court and their membership on the boards of legal
services organizations. So far they have remained aloof from the battle
because they are not involved in day-to-day administration and ordi-
narily do not care what happens as long as the corruption and mis-
management of the local political clubs do not become embarrassing,
or the reformers do not become too militant and alienate the Establishment. The poor themselves, I need hardly say, have no real power
over the program, and most so-called "representatives of the poor"
on local boards are usually quite conservative members of the bour-
geoisie.

The war between these two groups has been waged relentlessly
with neither side wholly prevailing, but the new political climate in
the country has recently added an ominous dimension to the conflict.
For the first time there is real doubt about the commitment of the
national administration to legal services. This has been made unmis-

---

29 See Pye, *The Role of Legal Services in the Antipoverty Program*, 31 LAW &
CONTEMP. PROB. 211, 247 (1966).

takenly evident by a series of recent decisions at the Office of Economic Opportunity, such as the apparent refusal to fund new research and development projects, the refusal to support a poverty public interest law firm after it was approved by the Director of Legal Services, and the plan to transfer a large measure of control of community action agencies from the federal government to state governors, where they will be vulnerable to political pressures. The new danger is best exemplified by a recent statement of Donald Rumsfeld, the Director of OEO, to a group of young poverty lawyers who had inquired if the independence of the legal services attorney-client relationship would be protected by OEO. Mr. Rumfeld replied as follows:

> Because legal services clients do not pay it is a fiction to say that a normal attorney-client relationship exists between the legal service lawyer and his client. You are responsible not only to your clients, but to this agency, Congress, and to the taxpayers of the United States.[30]

These words have a deceptively plausible ring. Certainly legal services lawyers have various responsibilities to OEO, Congress, and the taxpayers, but I fail to see why these responsibilities—that are chiefly fiscal and organizational—should dilute the traditional attorney-client relationship. If we permit this, surely the poor will be relegated to second-class citizenship before the law. In 1951 Learned Hand said, "If we are to keep our democracy, there must be one commandment: Thou shall not ration justice."[31] Thirty years earlier Charles Evans Hughes said that it is the obligation of lawyers to insure that "no man shall suffer in the enforcement of his legal rights for want of a skilled protector, able, fearless, and incorruptible."[32] I hope that we are not about to witness the erosion of these principles.

As I draw to a close I trust that my main message is evident—that lawyers face many open roads to public service, that any of those roads can lead to rewarding and, in the present state of our culture, vital professional destinies, and that the choice of route rests with each individual, who in the last analysis will be guided by his temperament, his philosophy, and his sense of the times. These are highly personal qualities and no speech, no exhortation, no incentive can replace the

---

30 Preliminary Report for 1969-70 of Alfred Feinberg, Chairman of PLEA (Poverty Lawyers for Effective Advocacy), undated. *See also* Christensen, *Give Us Don Baker Again*, 4 CLEARINGHOUSE REV. 51 (June 1970).
31 E. BROWNELL, *supra* note 3, at xviii.
32 Address by Charles Evans Hughes, American Bar Association Convention, 1920, in 45 ABA REP. 227, 234 (1920).

irreducible character and motivations of the individual man or woman. When the December of life approaches, as the psychologist Erik Erikson has written, there are those who will reap the joys of having lived an integrated and useful life, and others who will endure the shame and shadow of personal despair. I do not think that the role each lawyer plays in our turbulent ghetto society will be decisive in shaping his final state of mind, but neither do I believe that it will be irrelevant.

The Diminishing Right of Privacy:
The Personal Dossier
and the Computer

VERN COUNTRYMAN

The compiling of dossiers on individuals is not new in this country. The Federalists doubtless compiled dossiers on real and suspected Jacobins during the enforcement of the first Alien and Sedition Acts. After the prosecutions of suspects were completed, however, or at least when the Alien and Sedition Acts were repealed, those dossiers were apparently discarded.

As our numbers have increased and our society grown more complex, we have recognized ever more reasons—political, social, and economic—why one man has a "legitimate" interest in the affairs of another. For example, a company that contemplates extending credit to, insuring or employing John Doe asserts a "legitimate" interest in knowing something about his economic condition and often some of his other characteristics also. Responding to this asserted interest, an entire industry has developed to supply the needed information. And, because it is not efficient for a new compilation to be initiated every

VERN COUNTRYMAN, professor of law, Harvard University. Vern Countryman was born in Montana, and attended the University of Washington, where he received B.A. (1939) and LL.B. (1942) degrees. He also received the degree of M.A. (hon.) from Harvard University in 1964. His appointments have included assistant attorney general of the state of Washington (1946), assistant and then associate professor of law at Yale Law School (1948–1955), dean of the University of New Mexico School of Law (1959–1964), and professor of law at Harvard from 1964. He was also a Sterling Fellow of Yale. He has been legal consultant, Brookings Institution, Study of Bankruptcy; a member of the Consumer Bankruptcy Committee of the American Bar Association; and vice-chairman of the National Conference on Bankruptcy. His publications include *Debtors' and Creditors' Rights* (with Moore, 1951), *The Lawyer in Modern Society* (with Finman, 1966), and *Commercial Law* (with Kaufman, 1971). He is a member of the Washington, Maryland, Massachusetts, and District of Columbia bars.

time a new need arises, this industry maintains permanent dossiers on each of its subjects—dossiers whose final entries probably reflect not the death of the subjects, but the closing of the probate of their estates. Law enforcement agencies also profess a "legitimate" interest in compiling dossiers on suspected law violators. Here again, efficiency is interposed as a justification for maintaining the dossiers even after the case is closed.

Since World War II it has become fashionable to utilize a variety of prophylactic measures both to identify potential criminals before crimes are committed and to frustrate supposed intentions of potential criminals. These efforts include various loyalty programs, a bewildering variety of laws defining sedition and other political crimes, and the antics of legislative committees. To meet the "legitimate need" for the protection of government, many government agencies have gone into the business of compiling dossiers on the political beliefs, expressions, and associations of all those characterized as "subversive." Here, too, it is more efficient that these dossiers be permanent.

But the demands of that outstanding of all American virtues—efficiency—do not end here. Just as it is efficient for any one dossier compiler to maintain a permanent record on each subject, it is inefficient for another compiler not to utilize previous compilations. The drive for efficiency has inexorably led to a considerable interchange of data between compilers both within the generous limits allowed by law and sometimes beyond those limits.

The computer has further facilitated the quest for efficiency. With its endless capacity to store data and to regurgitate it with lightning-like speed, it is inefficient not to use the computer to combine the various dossiers compiled on each individual. If the present trend continues, the day will come when the push of a button will produce a complete "data profile" on each citizen, from his departure from the womb (or perhaps sometime earlier) to some time after he enters his tomb. While we cannot yet predict the precise arrival of this glorious day, there is enough available information to indicate the actuality of this trend and to provoke every concerned citizen to demand more information about and more protection against this development.

I. PRIVATELY COMPILED DOSSIERS

Within the private sector, the compilation of data on individuals is most frequently undertaken for profit, although the motivation is occasionally punitive or benevolent. Since Congress in recent years has investigated the operation of commercial agencies,[1] we are most knowledgeable about them. These commercial agencies fall into two categories: the credit bureau and the investigatory reporting agency.

A. The Commercial Compilers

In a very rough way, the credit bureau is to the user of consumer credit what Dun & Bradstreet's reporting service is to a business organization seeking credit. The credit bureau is not a new institution in our society, but as consumer credit has burgeoned by more than 2,000% in the past quarter century[2] so has the business of the credit bureau.

There are approximately 2,500 credit bureaus in the country, of which some 2,100 are members of one trade association, Associated Credit Bureaus, Inc. The files of bureaus affiliated with ACB include records on approximately 100 million persons, and those bureaus interchange their information.[3] The largest credit bureau operation outside the ACB is the Credit Data Corporation, which has files on 27 million persons.[4] While there is doubtless some overlap between the 100 million ACB files and the 27 million Credit Data Corporation files, the combined accumulation probably covers nearly all 131 million of us who are over eighteen years of age, particularly since most of the

---

1 There have been five separate Congressional hearings: *Hearings on Commercial Credit Bureaus Before the Spec. Subcomm. on Invasion of Privacy of the House Comm. on Gov't Operations*, 90th Cong., 2d Sess. (March 1968) [hereinafter cited as *House Credit Bureau Hearings I*]; *Hearings on Retail Credit Co. of Atlanta Before the Spec. Subcomm. on Invasion of Privacy of the House Comm. on Gov't Operations*, 90th Cong., 2d Sess. (May 1968) [hereinafter cited as *House Credit Bureau Hearings II*]; *Hearings on S. Res. 233 Before the Subcomm. on Antitrust and Monopoly of the Senate Judiciary Comm.*, 90th Cong., 2d Sess. (December 1968) [hereinafter cited as *Senate Credit Bureau Hearings I*]; *Hearings on S. 823 Before the Subcomm. on Financial Institutions of the Senate Banking and Currency Comm.*, 91st Cong., 1st Sess. (May 1969) [hereinafter cited as *Senate Credit Bureau Hearings II*]; *Hearings on H.R. 16340 Before the Subcomm. on Consumer Affairs of the House Comm. on Banking and Currency*, 91st Cong., 2d Sess. (March-April 1970) [hereinafter cited as *House Credit Bureau Hearings III*].

2 From $5.7 billion at the end of 1945 to $123.9 billion at the end of November 1970. FED. RESERVE BULL. A-54 (Jan. 1971).

3 ACB is also operating under a 1933 antitrust consent decree that requires the interchange of data with the 4000 credit bureaus not affiliated with it. *See* United States v. National Retail Credit Ass'n, Eq. No. 10420 (E.D. Mont., Oct. 6, 1933) (abstracted in AM. ENTERPRISE INSTITUTE FOR PUB. POLICY RESEARCH, ANTITRUST CONSENT DECREES 1906-1966, at 371 (1968)); *Senate Credit Bureau Hearings I, supra* note 1, at 23. In 1968 ACB entered into arrangements with International Telephone & Telegraph Corporation to provide a computer service to facilitate the interchange. *Id.* at 24, 33-34.

4 In November 1969 all of the stock of Credit Data Corp. was acquired by TRW Credit Information Services, Inc., which now operates the Credit reporting service as TRW Credit Data. *House Credit Bureau Hearings III, supra* note 1, at 156. This bureau is completely computerized and is adding files at the rate of one-half million per month. *House Credit Bureau Hearings III, supra* note 1, at 157, 165; *Senate Credit Bureau Hearings II, supra* note 1, at 223, 227.

93 million of us who are married will be combined in some 46 million files with our spouses.[5]

The content and the reliability of information in credit bureau files is dictated largely by the three principal sources from which the credit bureaus draw. A principal source of information is the bureau's own subscribers, the merchants, banks and finance companies who buy most of the credit reports. They supply information on their own customers with regard to employment, approximate income and credit performance. The value of this source is subject to three significant limitations. First, since the credit bureau files do not reveal the subject's net worth, or even his state of solvency, but only whether his accounts with the bureau's subscribers are delinquent, the extension of credit in reliance on a credit bureau report proceeds on the illogical assumption that the ability to meet current credit payments betokens the capacity to handle one additional debt. Second, credit bureau files cannot even approximate the amount of a subject's debts, since many creditors are not subscribers. Third, the delinquency of an account frequently results not from financial irresponsibility but from a bona fide dispute over the amount owing or the quality of merchandise sold.

As a second source of information, the more enterprising bureaus scrutinize official records for arrests, lawsuits, judgments, bankruptcies, mortgages, tax liens, marriages, divorces, births and deaths. The substantial possibility of mistaken identity, combined with the frequent failure of official records to include final dispositions, renders this source highly unreliable. As a third source of information, most credit bureaus also maintain a news-clipping service, although this occasionally serves as a substitute for checking official records. Obviously, this source poses even greater danger of error than the official record check with regard to mistaken identity or the failure to note the ultimate disposition of arrests, lawsuits, judgments and liens.

During Congressional hearings on the subject, much attention was focused on the denial of credit due to erroneous adverse information in credit bureau files. Unstressed but equally serious is the erroneous extension of credit. Just as mistaken identity leads to the insertion of data in an inappropriate file, so also its leads to the omission of relevant information from the appropriate file. And few, if any, files will record all debts. Inaccurate files thus mean that credit is both erroneously denied and granted. In their own defense, credit bureaus

---

[5] U.S. BUREAU OF THE CENSUS, STATISTICAL ABSTRACT OF THE UNITED STATES 25, 32 (1970).

stress that they only collate information and that they never claim to make affirmative investigations of their subjects.[6]

It is no coincidence that, as consumer credit expanded by more than 2,000% in the past twenty-five years, so did consumer bankruptcies—from 8,500 in 1946 to 178,000 in 1970.[7] If a credit extender were to compare the report he received from the credit bureau with the debts scheduled by a subject in his bankruptcy proceeding, he might conclude that the credit report was not worth the 35 to 75 cents paid for it.[8] Upon entries of such fragile reliability is your "credit rating" built. And when the credit bureaus also engage in debt collection—and many of them do, finding their ability to affect the credit rating an effective collection tool[9]— the reliability of the entries is even further threatened by a built-in conflict of interest.

Credit bureau files are thus inadequate to satisfy some who contemplate commercial relationships. In consequence, prospective employers and insurers often turn for information to the investigatory reporting agency.[10] Congressional committees heard from representatives of the largest of such agencies in this country—Retail Credit Company of Atlanta, with 1,225 offices, 7,000 inspectors, and files on 48 million persons.[11] Inspectors from Retail Credit not only check

---

6 On occasion, however, bureaus join with local merchants in sponsoring the Welcome Wagon lady who reports back to the merchants on the apparent worldly needs of the newcomers she visits and to the credit bureau on their apparent credit worthiness—and on where the newcomer came from, so that his file can be obtained from a credit bureau at his former location. *Senate Credit Bureau Hearings II, supra* note 1, at 119, 167-172; *House Credit Bureau Hearings III, supra* note 1, at 33.

7 Ad. Office of United States Courts, Tables of Bankrupcy Statistics, Table F-3 (1946); Ad. Office of United States Courts, Ann. Rep. of the Director, V-4 (1970).

8 This is the price the subscriber pays to learn what reposes in the compiler's file at the moment he makes inquiry. If he wants the file brought up to date by calls to other subscribers he must pay an additional fee. Save for routine checking of public records and newspaper clippings, the files are not updated until a subscriber requests, and pays for, that action.

In hearings held in Washington, D.C. in March, 1968, a New York Congressman asked for a demonstration of Credit Data Corporation's high-speed computerized retrieval of his New York City credit file. Within the time consumed by six pages of printed hearing record, the report came back on one bank loan as of June, 1967, and nothing else. The Congressman's response: "A very inefficient system, thank God." *House Credit Bureau Hearings I, supra* note 1, at 72-79.

9 *Senate Credit Bureau Hearings I, supra* note 1, at 5, 23, 28-30, 40-43, 45, 53, 78; *Senate Credit Bureau Hearings II, supra* note 1, at 180.

10 Two of the subcommittees also heard testimony from representatives of one agency specializing in reports on prospective mortgagors to banks and institutional lenders. Their testimony was to the effect that they confined their investigation to public records and newspaper clippings, did not engage in "questioning neighbors," and always gave the subject an opportunity to explain adverse items of public record or news report—unless the client asked them not to contact the subject or unless the client asked for a quick, telephone report on what the files contained. *Senate Credit Bureau Hearings II, supra* note 1, at 237-254; *House Credit Bureau Hearings III, supra* note 1, at 211-230.

11 *Senate Credit Bureau Hearings II, supra* note 1, at 175; *House Credit Bureau Hearings III, supra* note 1, at 473-474.

public records and clip newspapers, but also interview friends, neighbors, former neighbors, acquaintances, employers, former employers, business associates—anyone who may know something, or have an opinion, about the subject.[12] For life insurance companies Retail Credit inspectors inquire about the subject's drinking habits and domestic difficulties, seek out criticism of his character and morals, and report whether his living conditions are crowded or dirty.[13] For automobile insurers Retail Credit investigates the subject's neighborhood business reputation, morals, and "antagonistic-antisocial conduct."[14] For employers, Retail Credit's inspectors also report whether the subject has any "known connection with a 'peace movement' or any other organization of a subversive type" and whether he is reputed to be "neurotic or psychotic."[15]

In response to Congressional concern about the reliability of agency reports, spokesmen for Retail Credit proffered two assurances. First, its inspectors are carefully trained persons of "unusual inspection ability."[16] This assurance lost some of its force when inquiry revealed that these highly qualified, well-trained inspectors commanded a starting salary of $475 to $500 per month, that they prepared anywhere from 2 to 16 reports per day, that half had no more than a high school education, and that another 30% were college dropouts.[17] Second, Retail Credit reported that adverse information not coming from public records either is confirmed from a second source or is reported as unconfirmed.[18] Whatever comfort otherwise might be drawn from this assurance is somewhat qualified by evidence to the contrary.[19]

---

12 *House Credit Bureau Hearings II, supra* note 1, at 21; *Senate Credit Bureau Hearings I, supra* note 1, at 108.

13 *Senate Credit Bureau Hearings II, supra* note 1, at 196-203.

14 The auto insurers are convinced that there is some correlation between all of these factors (except antagonistic-antisocial conduct) and accident frequency, and that both immorality and antagonistic-antisocial conduct would impair the subject's effectiveness as a witness in the event of litigation. *Senate Credit Bureau Hearings II, supra* note 1, at 207-212, 305-316; *House Credit Bureau Hearings III, supra* note 1, at 514-516. The latter consideration, of course, should dictate an inquiry into hare-lips, unsightly scars and birthmarks, and the use of deodorants.

15 *Senate Credit Bureau Hearings I, supra* note 1, at 109-110; *Senate Credit Bureau Hearings II, supra* note 1, at 176-177.

16 *House Credit Bureau Hearings II, supra* note 1, at 19-20; see also *Senate Credit Bureau Hearings II, supra* note 1, at 175-176.

17 *Senate Credit Bureau Hearings II, supra* note 1, at 176, 192; *House Credit Bureau Hearings III, supra* note 1, at 473, 503.

18 *House Credit Bureau Hearings II, supra* note 1, at 21; *House Credit Bureau Hearings III, supra* note 1 at 474.

19 One well-trained, highly-qualified inspector, who heard from two sources that a subject had served in prison, reported the prison record as an unqualified fact although the inspector found no confirmation in court or prison records. *Wagner v. Retail Credit Co.*, 338 F.2d 598 (7th Cir. 1964).

Access to the files of these commercial compilers is reportedly restricted to "reputable" business organizations that possess a "legitimate" business interest.[20] However, Congressional and private inquiry has undercut this assertion and ably demonstrated the easy availability of the files, not only to private parties[21] but also to government agencies.[22]

---

20 *House Credit Bureau Hearings I, supra* note 1, at 63-64, 90; *House Credit Bureau Hearings II, supra* note 1, at 19; *Senate Credit Bureau Hearings I, supra* note 1, at 62.

21 Credit bureau spokesmen have admitted the possibility of an employee of a credit bureau subscriber obtaining a report for purposes unrelated to his employer's business. *House Credit Bureau Hearings I, supra* note 1, at 111; *Senate Credit Bureau Hearings II, supra* note 1, at 228. Retail Credit's spokesmen admitted that it sometimes gave out reports as a "favor" when, for example, an executive of a subscriber asked for a report on a man being considered as a new minister for his church. *House Credit Bureau Hearings II, supra* note 1, at 19, 38; *Senate Credit Bureau Hearings I, supra* note 1, at 101.

Moreover, the compilers had been under interrogation by Congressional committees for over a year when CBS News conducted an experiment. Using a fictitious company name, it sent out twenty letters to credit bureaus requesting reports on named individuals. It received ten reports and offers of two more if it would sign a subscriber's contract. On a second effort, the fictitious company sent out twenty-eight letters. This time it did not state that it was considering granting credit—it simply asked for a full credit report, without stating why it wanted it. And this time it asked only about individuals who had been complaining to Congressional committees about the credit bureaus. This time it received only seven of the requested reports—plus one more when it accepted the offer of one credit bureau to sign a subscriber's contract. *Senate Credit Bureau Hearings II, supra* note 1, at 378-381; *House Credit Bureau Hearings III, supra* note 1, at 59-61.

22 This includes not only such governmental credit-granting agencies as the Federal Housing Administration and the Veterans Administration, which buy such reports just as do private subscribers. It includes also such law enforcement agencies as the FBI and the Internal Revenue Service. Members of ACB and the Retail Credit Company make their files available to the law-enforcers "as a public service." *House Credit Bureau Hearings I, supra* note 1, at 134-138; *House Credit Bureau Hearings II, supra* note 1, at 23, 39; *Senate Credit Bureau Hearings II, supra* note 1, at 149, 161; *House Credit Bureau Hearings III, supra* note 1, at 603, 605. The Credit Data Corporation took a different view, and refused to turn over its reports to the IRS. *House Credit Bureau Hearings I, supra* note 1, at 90-91; *Senate Credit Bureau Hearings I, supra* note 1, at 62-63. It was then met with a statutory summons calling for all credit information relative to named taxpayers. The IRS is authorized, for the purposes of "determining the liability of any person for any internal revenue tax" to summon the taxpayer "or any other person the [IRS] may deem proper," to produce "such books, papers, records, or other data . . . as may be relevant or material to such inquiry . . . ." INT. REV. CODE OF 1954, § 7602. When Credit Data refused to obey the summons, IRS got a judicial order of enforcement pursuant to the statute, requiring it to comply on payment by the IRS of 75 cents per report, the fee which Credit Data charged its regular subscribers. On appeal, Credit Data won a great victory. The decision below was affirmed in all respects save that the case was remanded to determine the "fair value" which IRS must pay for the reports—the rate paid by subscribers was not to be taken as conclusive because subscribers supply "valuable credit information" to Credit Data. United States v. Davey, 426 F.2d 842, 844 (2d Cir. 1970).

The result was foreshadowed by previous decisions of the Supreme Court. In a long line of cases that court has sustained judicial enforcement of an administrative agency's statutory subpoenas against fourth amendment attack where the subpoena sought testimony about the affairs or the records of the person subpoenaed, if the subpoena was sufficiently specific to satisfy the fourth amendment, if the administrative inquiry was authorized by Congress, and if the evidence sought was relevant to the inquiry—the court's application of the last two requirements when its enforcement order was sought being held to satisfy the fourth amendment's requirement of probable cause. United States v. Morton Salt Co., 338 U.S. 632 (1950); Oklahoma Press Publishing Co. v. Walling, 327 U.S. 186 (1946). Earlier decisions are discussed in 1 K. DAVIS, ADMINISTRATIVE LAW TREATISE § 3.12 (1958) and Comment, *Agency Access to Credit Bureau Files: Federal Invasion of Privacy?* 12 B.C. IND. & COM. L. REV. 110, 113-118 (1970). More than forty-five years ago the Supreme Court also

Notwithstanding the otherwise easy accessibility of files, commercial compilers steadfastly refuse to permit the subject to see the file. Three reasons are given for this position—one laughable and two believable. First, if the subject ever got his hands on the file, even in the compiler's office, he might destroy it. Second, to let the subject see the file would be to reveal the compiler's sources and would tend to "dry up" those sources.[23] Third, if the file consists of a computer printout, the subject wouldn't be able to understand it.[24]

As a consequence of past practices, many subjects do not know that a denial of credit, employment or insurance may be caused by an adverse report from a commercial compiler. Even the individual who is aware of that fact, and who believes that the adverse report is erroneous, seldom can obtain legal relief. If he sues on a theory of defamation or interference with economic expectations, he encounters the defense of qualified privilege: the subscriber's "legitimate" interest in the subject's affairs protects the compiler who avoids gross negligence or malice.[25] If the subject resorts to an action for invasion of privacy, he confronts the traditional assertion[26] that the right to privacy proscribes only *publicizing* private matters. Even if he persuades a court

---

summarily affirmed a decision that no fourth amendment question was even presented when the IRS, investigating the tax liability of a bank depositor, summoned the bank to produce its records. First National Bank of Mobile v. United States, 267 U.S. 576 (1925). Since the Credit Data case was decided, the Supreme Court has unanimously extended that ruling to cover an IRS summons to the taxpayer's employer and, by dictum, to any other third person with no established legal privilege, such as an attorney, where the taxpayer has "no proprietary interest of any kind" in the records subpoenaed. *See* Donaldson v. United States, 91 S. Ct. 534, 538 (1971) (taxpayer sought to intervene in the enforcement proceeding against the employer, but was held not to have a sufficient interest to entitle him to do so.); *cf.* Reisman v. Caplin, 375 U.S. 440 (1964). The fourth amendment, therefore, offers no apparent protection to the subject whose file in a credit bureau is subjected to an administrative subpoena or summons of a governmental agency showing a "legitimate" interest in its contents.

[23] Doubtless this reason should be expanded to say that the nondisclosure of the files protects not only the compiler's sources, but also the compiler himself from trouble (including litigation) with the subject.

[24] *See House Credit Bureau Hearings I, supra* note 1, at 97; *House Credit Bureau Hearings II, supra* note 1, at 13-16; *Senate Credit Bureau Hearings I, supra* note 1, at 21-22, 114-115; *Senate Credit Bureau Hearings II, supra* note 1, at 153, 173, 179, 232-233, 270; *House Credit Bureau Hearings III, supra* note 1, at 160, 168, 460-461, 466-467, 490.

[25] *See* Roemer v. Retail Credit Co., 3 Cal. App. 3d 368, 83 Cal. Reptr. 540 (1970); Karst, *"The Files": Legal Controls Over the Accuracy and Accessibility of Stored Personal Data,* 31 LAW & CONTEMP. PROB. 342, 345-347 (1966); Comment, *Credit Investigations and The Right to Privacy: Quest for a Remedy,* 57 GEO. L.J. 509, 513-523 (1959). The first amendment protection accorded defamatory but nonmalicious news stories about public figures by New York Times Co. v. Sullivan, 376 U.S. 254 (1964), has been held not to extend to private subscription credit reports. Grove v. Dun & Bradstreet, Inc., 438 F.2d 433 (3d Cir. 1971).

[26] For the famous law review article that launched this concept into American jurisprudence see Warren & Brandeis, *The Right to Privacy,* 4 HARV. L. REV. 193 (1890). *See also* Kalven, *Privacy in Tort Law—Were Warren and Brandeis Wrong?,* 31 LAW & CONTEMP. PROB. 326 (1966).

that the concept has developed to protect against all offensive intrusions into private affairs,[27] the court may respond that this right is qualified by the "legitimate" interest of the user of the files.[28]

Notwithstanding this lack of judicial empathy, Congressional investigators were sympathetic to individuals whose dossiers contained erroneous adverse information. The result was enactment[29] of the Fair Credit Reporting Act of 1970.[30] The Act applies only to the accuracy and accessibility of the reports. No attempt is made to limit the nature of their contents. The report which the Act reaches, whether issued by

---

[27] *See* 1 F. HARPER & F. JAMES, THE LAW OF TORTS § 9.6 (1956); W. PROSSER, THE LAW OF TORTS § 112 (3d ed. 1964).

[28] Shorter v. Retail Credit Co., 251 F. Supp. 329 (D.S.C. 1966); Comment, *Credit Investigations and The Right to Privacy: Quest for a Remedy*, 57 GEO. L.J. 509, 523-527 (1969).

[29] The compilers detected this Congressional sentiment and decided that if they could not fight the move for reform, they had better join the effort in hope of obtaining a palatable result. *See* Denney, *Federal Fair Credit Reporting Act*, 25 PERS. FIN. LAW Q. REP. 4 (1970). *See also House Credit Bureau Hearings III, supra* note 1, at 108.

[30] 84 Stat. 1114, tit. VI (1970 U.S. CODE CONG. & AD. NEWS 5142). This Act, applicable both to credit bureaus and to investigatory reporting agencies, attempts to guard against inaccurate or stale information in their reports and to restrict the use of the reports by provisions that:
  (1) Require the compilers to maintain "reasonable procedures" to eliminate from their reports bankruptcies after 14 years and other adverse information after 7 years.
  (2) Require the employers to keep their public record entries in employment reports up to date to the extent that the public records are up to date, and require the investigatory agencies to confirm their adverse interview information at least 3 months before reporting it.
  (3) Require users of investigatory reports to notify the subject that such a report is being made; require users of credit or investigatory reports to advise the subject whenever credit, insurance or employment is denied, "wholly or partly because of" the report and to identify the reporting agency; and require compilers reporting adverse public record information for employment purposes to advise the subject of that fact.
  (4) Require any compiler, on request of a subject, to disclose to him the "nature and substance" of the information on him in its files (but not the file itself); require credit bureau compilers to disclose also the sources of their data; and require all compilers to reinvestigate any item which the subject disputes and, if it does not correct the item, to include in future reports his statement of not more than 100 words describing the dispute unless the compiler has "reasonable grounds to believe" the statement is "frivolous or irrelevant."
  (5) Require the compilers to maintain "reasonable procedures" to confine the furnishing of their reports, without written consent of the subject, to those who have "a legitimate business need" for them.
  (6) Forbid compilers, without written consent of the subject, to furnish more than name, address and place of employment of a subject to a governmental agency except in connection with licensing, governmental grants or other business transactions where the government has a "legitimate business need"—and except in response to court order.
  (7) Authorize damage actions for subjects when there is negligence in failing to comply with the Act, punitive damages for wilful noncompliance with the Act, and administrative enforcement by the FTC.
  (8) Immunize compilers and their sources of information from any other liability save for false information "furnished with malice or wilful intent to injure" the subject.
  (9) Impose criminal penalties for officers or employees of compilers who "knowingly and wilfully" make unauthorized disclosures of information and for any person who "knowingly and wilfully" obtains such information "under false pretenses."

a credit bureau or an investigatory agency, is defined to mean any communication bearing not only on credit, but also on "character, general reputation, personal characteristics, or mode of living."

B. The Punitive Compilers

There has been no official investigation of those private compilers who assemble dossiers for the purpose of punishing those with whom they disagree. Nonetheless, it is safe to generalize that the punitive compilers are sponsored and staffed by right-wing extremists. This is not to say that right-wing extremists are more (or less, depending upon your point of view) lacking in virtue than left-wing extremists. The explanation derives from the fact that official investigations of extremist groups have almost invariably focused on those on the left end of the political spectrum (although they tend to hit anyone to the left of the right-wing extremists). Hence, since private punitive compilers rely almost entirely upon official investigations as their sources of information, there is not enough available information to compile dossiers on right-wing extremists. Moreover, in the absence of official investigations to whet the public interest, there would be no substantial market for dossiers on right-wing extremists even if they could be compiled.

Some punitive compilers, like American Business Consultants, operate for profit. Organized by three former FBI agents, this group operated during the heyday of Senator Joseph McCarthy. It published the newsletter *Counterattack*, which provided dossiers on those not sufficiently anti-Communist, with special emphasis on the news media, writers and publishers, and *Red Channels*, which focussed on those similarly lacking in the entertainment business.[31] Other punitive compilers, like the Americanism Committees of some American Legion posts, the John Birch Society, and Aware, Inc. operate out of their own versions of patriotism.

The punitive compilers' principal aim is to deprive the subject of his employment. Since their dossiers are neither solicited nor often wanted by employers, the "legitimate" needs of the employer cannot be justifiably invoked as a defense to a defamation or an invasion of privacy action. Offsetting their apparent legal vulnerability is the fact that most, if not all, of the punitive compilers are either completely

---

31 *See* M. MILLER, The JUDGES AND THE JUDGED (1952).

judgment proof or incapable of responding in damages for the full injury caused.[32]

C. The Benevolent Compilers

Many of those who compile personal dossiers, or who support their compilation, are interested not in the individual subjects but in groups. Included in this category are the government officials and business executives who seek to make informed decisions and plans, and the scholars (particularly the social scientists) who seek to aid decision making and planning. Although the interest is confined to groups, it is inescapable that information about groups must come from, and relate to, individuals.

At first blush it might seem that group information could be obtained and compiled without preserving a record of the identity of the component individuals. Unfortunately, some key to the identity of the subjects must be retained if group compilations are to be kept current and if the compilations are to be available for new uses. So long as keys to the identity of those in the group are retained, these compilations provide a potential source of personal dossiers, either as a consequence of unauthorized use or as a consequence of a change in the policy of the compilers. Unfortunately, many of those who use group compilations are so single-mindedly devoted to their own purposes that they are heedless of this danger. Thus, a committee of the Social Science Research Council in 1965 proposed that the Bureau

---

[32] Both of these facts were dramatically demonstrated by a distinguished and courageous graduate of the University of Texas, John Henry Faulk. He lost his position with CBS in 1956 as a consequence of a publication of a dossier—largely based on erroneous information in the files of the House Un-American Activities Committee—in a bulletin published by Aware, Inc. In part, also, the loss of his job was due to an advertising boycott launched by the owner of a chain of grocery supermarkets after the bulletin was published. Faulk sued Aware, one of its employees and the supermarket owner for libel, realizing that Aware and its employee were not capable of responding in damages in any sufficient amount. After a trial in which the court ruled that the defense of qualified privilege was not available and that defendants had failed to prove the defense of truth, the jury returned a verdict for $3,500,000—of which $1,000,000 was actual damages against all three defendants, $1,250,000 was punitive damages against Aware, and $1,250,000 was punitive damages against its employee. There was no award of punitive damages against the supermarket owner because, unfortunately, he died shortly before the case went to the jury. The judgment against him was settled with his disappointingly small estate for $175,000. After an appeal by the surviving defendants in which they were castigated as "malicious" and "vicious" purveyors of libel, the judgment was reduced to $400,000 total actual damages, $50,000 punitive damages against Aware and $100,000 punitive damages against its employee, no part of which was collectible from Aware or its employee. Faulk v. Aware, Inc. 19 App. Div. 2d 464, 244 N.Y.S.2d 259 (1963), *aff'd*, 14 N.Y.S.2d 899, 200 N.E.2d 778, 252 N.Y.S.2d 95 (1964), *cert. denied*, 380 U.S. 916 (1965). *See also* J. FAULK, FEAR ON TRIAL (1964). Faulk's attorney has also written about the case in his usual self-effacing manner. *See* L. NIZER, THE JURY RETURNS 225-438 (1966). Neither book reveals how much of the $175,000 actually collected went to Faulk.

of the Budget establish a National Data Center to collect and computerize all machine-readable data of all federal agencies for use both by the government and by individual scholars. The report was eloquent on the "efficiency" of such an operation, but took account of the threat to individual privacy only to the extent of suggesting that when a government agency has obtained data under a pledge of confidentiality, "it is often possible to disguise the information in such a way that specific data cannot be traced to any individual respondent."[33]

A personal experience provides another illustration of the scholar's insensitivity to problems of privacy where his thirst for knowledge is concerned. Early in 1969, a private foundation sent out a questionnaire to university graduate students seeking their opinions on a variety of subjects ranging from drug use to forcible overthrow of the government. Since the students were instructed to return these questionnairses with their names on them, one graduate student called me to ask if there was any danger, despite the foundation's assurance of confidentiality, that his replies might come into the hands of a government agency. My advice, subsequently printed in the *Harvard Crimson*, was that the foundation would have no defense to an administrative or legislative subpoena. I thereupon received a lengthy letter from a Harvard professor of government taking me to task. First, he explained to me that he had nothing to do with the particular questionnaire but assured me, based on his thirty-five years of experience, that it was "typical of those used by both academic and commercial pollsters." Second, he explained to me—not quite as adequately as I have explained to you—why the identity of those polled must be preserved. Third, he expressed doubt that any government agency would seek to obtain the information. Fourth, though he was not a lawyer, he ventured the opinion that the courts would very likely create some sort of

---

[33] The report is printed in *Hearings on the Computer and Invasion of Privacy Before the Spec. Subcomm. on Invasion of Privacy of the House Comm. on Gov't Operations*, 89th Cong., 2d Sess., ser. 1, pt. 1, at 195, 202.

The Bureau referred the report for review to a research analyst employed by Resources for the Future, Inc., a private foundation. He endorsed the proposal in a report much concerned with organizational and operational problems but which did not mention problems of privacy. *Id.* at 254. The Bureau next created a task force, consisting of one statistician and five academicians, to consider the problem. The task force also endorsed the proposed National Data Center, but its report took account of hearings on the subject wherein congressmen had been highly critical of the danger to privacy. The task force took this criticism rather lightly, however, since it thought that Congress could define a standard for access to the data in the center that could be enforced and that the technical possibility that the federal computers might themselves be tapped by technological means could be met by unspecified "organizational and technical means . . . available to control and limit the risks." This report is printed in *Hearings on S. Res. 25 on Computer Privacy Before the Subcomm. on Ad. Practice & Procedure of the Senate Judiciary Comm.*, 90th Cong., 1st Sess., ser. 1, pt. 1, at 25, 37 (1967).

privilege to block a government subpoena. Fifth, he pointed out that advice such as mine might well reduce the number of responses to the questionnaire. Finally, he urged me to reconsider and to issue another statement on the matter. I declined his invitation on the grounds that I thought my legal advice was better than his and that the students were entitled to have that advice so that they, rather than he, I, or the foundation, could do their own speculating about the likelihood of a government subpoena.

This is not to suggest that all group compilers are insensitive to the privacy problem or to the danger that the compilations might provide a source for personal dossiers. But, even awareness of this danger betokens only the intention, not the ability, to safeguard the compilations. Once the data has been amassed, even the best intentioned compiler can do little more than attempt to guard the identity of subjects and hope that his successors in control of the compilation will be similarly sensitive to the danger.[34]

II. Publicly Compiled Dossiers

If information on private compilers of dossiers is incomplete, the information available on governmental compilers is fragmentary. The little that is known is based on disclosures made by the news media and on sporadic hearings conducted by Senate subcommittees.

Since the government can compel the subject to provide information about himself, the government has a unique source of information. In addition, governmental compilers also rely, as does the Retail Credit Company, on the personal interviewing of neighbors, associates, and acquaintances of the subject. Although government investigators are better paid, and hopefully better qualified and trained, than private inspectors, the difference may not be enough to inspire great confidence in the objectivity of their work product.[35]

---

[34] The problem is well illustrated by the United Planing Organization (UPO) of Washington, D.C., a private organization devoted to combatting problems of poverty. In the course of its work, UPO has found it useful to compile data from public records on such matters as juvenile arrests, school dropouts, evictions and welfare payments. To guard the identity of its subjects, UPO transferred all of its data to a trustee under an irrevocable trust with strictures which permit UPO to have continued access to it only so long as it does not reveal the identity of its subjects. *Hearings on S. Res. 25 on Computer Privacy Before the Subcomm. on Ad. Practice & Procedure of the Senate Judiciary Comm.*, 90th Cong., 2d Sess., ser. 16, pt. 2, at 309-317 (1968). Under the terms of the trust, UPO apparently will indeed lose access to the data if it changes its policy and discloses the identity of its subjects or, possibly, if one of its officers or employees makes an unauthorized disclosure. But, by that time, personal dossiers on all of its subjects may be in someone else's computer.

[35] Those in academic life are familiar with the FBI agent and the military investigator who comes to inquire about former students seeking government employment or a military commission. Most would agree that there is no faster way to get the visitor out of the

A. Government's Power—Legal and Otherwise

Governmental compilers have another source of information disclaimed by Retail Credit Company: wiretapping and electronic bugging.[36] Because of what it reveals, with regard both to governmental attitudes toward individual privacy and to the feasibility of legislative efforts to protect privacy, it will be instructive to survey briefly the history of the use of these devices.

In 1928 the Supreme Court held that government wiretapping did not violate the fourth amendment.[37] In the Communications Act of 1934 Congress made it a crime for anyone, without authority of the sender, wilfully to intercept any communication by wire or radio and to divulge the contents of the intercepted communication to any other person.[38] Thereafter, the Court held that because a wiretap was illegal, evidence so obtained,[39] including the "fruit of the poisonous tree,"[40] was inadmissible in federal courts. Despite the clear holding that federal agents commit a federal crime when they tap telephones, the FBI has, with Presidential approval, continued to engage in wiretapping.[41]

---

office than to make clear that you have nothing derogatory to say about the subject. And I can testify from my own experience that the visitor will depart almost as rapidly if, in a case where you have something to say which might conceivably be considered derogatory, you tell the visitor you want your secretary to take down your statement so that you can send a copy to the subject.

[36] Spokesmen for Retail Credit Co. emphatically and repeatedly deny resorting to such methods. *See House Credit Bureau Hearings II, supra* note 1, at 16; *Senate Credit Bureau Hearings I, supra* note 1, at 101; *Senate Credit Bureau Hearings II, supra* note 1, at 180; *House Credit Bureau Hearings III, supra* note 1, at 473.

[37] Olmstead v. United States, 277 U.S. 438 (1928).

[38] 47 U.S.C. §§ 501, 605 (1964).

[39] Nardone v. United States, 302 U.S. 379 (1937). *See also* Weiss v. United States, 308 U.S. 321 (1939).

[40] Nardone v. United States, 308 U.S. 338 (1939).

[41] The FBI commenced the practice in 1931 and continued until March 1940, when Attorney General Jackson ordered it stopped, admitting that it was illegal. Brownell, *The Public Security and Wire Tapping*, 39 CORN. L.Q. 195, 197-199 (1954). Emerson & Haber, *Reply by the Authors*, 58 YALE L.J. 412, 414-415 (1949). In May 1940, however, President Roosevelt issued a secret directive, the existence of which was not made public until after his death, ordering wiretapping resumed against "persons suspected of subversive activities against the Government of the United States, including suspected spies." Brief of the United States at Appendix A, United States v. Dellinger, No. 69CR180 (N.D. Ill., Feb. 20, 1970); Theoharis & Meyers, *The "National Security" Justification for Electronic Eavesdropping: An Elusive Exception*, 14 WAYNE L. REV. 749, 759 (1968); Rogers, *The Case for Wire Tapping*, 63 YALE L.J. 793, 795 (1954); *Rejoinder by Mr. Hoover*, 58 YALE L.J. 422, 423 (1949). Thereafter, Attorney General Biddle in 1941 announced that the Department of Justice intended to use wire tapping in "espionage, sabotage, and kidnapping cases when the circumstances warranted," and President Truman in 1947 approved the use of wire tapping "in cases vitally affecting the domestic security, or where human life is in jeopardy." Brief of United States at Appendix B, United States v. Dellinger, No. 69CR180 (N.D. Ill. Feb. 20, 1970); Rogers, *supra* at 798. In 1964 President Johnson issued a directive forbidding wire tapping by federal agents, except in national security cases. And in 1965 Attorney General Katzenbach testified that, "under present law, [wire tapping] should be permitted only where national security is involved" and acknowledged that the department had 62 wiretaps then

The practice of electronic bugging has been governed by a series of decisions holding that the fourth amendment is not violated by the interception of communications by means of detectaphones or informers wired for sound, so long as the interception is accomplished without a physical trespass.[42]

Regardless of the state of the law or of the current content of executive directives, FBI Director Hoover has annually since 1965 assured the House Appropriations Committee that every wiretap undertaken by the FBI has been "approved in advance and in writing by the Attorney General" and that all taps were limited to "national security" or "internal security" cases.[43] But less than two months after he gave that testimony in 1969 an FBI agent testified in the trial of Cassius Clay that the FBI had tapped the wires of Martin Luther King for four years before his death in 1968.[44] Hoover then produced his version of an "approval in writing in advance by the Attorney General" —a memorandum written by one of Hoover's own subordinates, reciting that in 1963 Attorney General Robert Kennedy, now also deceased, had inquired "if it was feasible to use electronic devices" to

---

in effect "under my specific direction." *Hearings on S. Res. 39 on Invasion of Privacy (Gov't Agencies) Before the Subcomm. on Ad. Practice & Procedure of the Senate Judiciary Committee*, 89th Cong., 1st Sess., ser. 38, pt. 3, at 1155, 1641 (1965). In 1967 Attorney General Ramsey Clark issued a memorandum requiring prior written approval of the Attorney General for any federal wiretap or electronic bugging save in "national security" cases, which "shall continue to be taken up directly with the Attorney General in the light of existing stringent restrictions." Theoharis & Meyers, *supra* at 755-756. Since the Communications Act contains no exceptions, it is quite clear that the Department of Justice has been violating that Act for most of the time since its enactment. From time to time spokesmen for the Department have made the argument that the contents of wiretaps are not "divulged"—and hence the Communications Act is not violated—where the contents are merely communicated from one federal agent to another. Katzenbach, *An Approach to the Problems of Wiretapping*, 32 F.R.D. 107 (1963); Brownell, *supra* at 198. But this proposition has never been tested in the courts—the Department of Justice has never seen fit to prosecute an FBI agent or any other federal agent for violation of the Communications Act, even in cases where convictions of others have been reversed because the contents of wiretaps were divulged in court.

42 Osborn v. United States, 385 U.S. 323 (1966); Lopez v. United States, 373 U.S. 427 (1963); On Lee v. United States, 343 U.S. 747 (1952); Goldman v. United States, 316 U.S. 129 (1942); *cf.* Silverman v. United States, 365 U.S. 505 (1960) (use of "spike mike" in party wall held a forbidden physical trespass).

43 *Hearings on Dep't of Justice Appropriations for 1970 Before a Subcomm. of the House Comm. on Appropriations*, 91st Cong., 1st Sess., 544 (1969); *Hearings on Dep't of Justice Appropriations for 1969 Before a Subcomm. of the House Comm. on Appropriations*, 90th Cong., 2d Sess., 549 (1968); *Hearings on Dep't of Justice Appropriations for 1968 Before a Subcomm. of the House Comm. on Appropriations*, 90th Cong., 1st Sess., 626 (1967); *Hearings on Dep't of Justice Appropriations for 1967 Before a Subcomm. of the House Comm. on Appropriations*, 89th Cong., 2d Sess., 262 (1966); *Hearings on Dep't of Justice Appropriations for 1966 Before a Subcomm. of the House Comm. on Appropriations*, 89th Cong., 1st Sess., 323 (1965).

44 N.Y. Times, June 5, 1969, at 27, col. 1. *See also* United States v. Clay, 430 F.2d 165 (5th Cir. 1970), *cert. granted*, 91 S. Ct. 457 (1971). Later testimony in the same trial revealed that the FBI had also tapped the wires of Black Muslim leader Elijah Muhammad from 1962 until 1966. N.Y. Times, June 8, 1969, at 29, col. 1.

check into allegations that King "had Marxist leanings."[45] The House
Appropriations Committee found no reason to question Hoover's
credibility when he appeared before it the following year and again
testified that "all" wiretaps "were authorized in advance in writing by
the Attorney General."[46]

Meanwhile, both constitutional and statutory requirements applicable to wiretapping and electronic bugging had changed. In 1967 the
Court in *Berger v. New York*[47] invalidated a New York statute that authorized electronic bugging with prior court approval when physical
trespass was involved, because the statute did not satisfy the fourth
amendment's requirements[48] of specificity as to the crime involved
or the conversations to be overheard. Later in the same year, in *Katz v.
United States*,[49] the Court concluded that the fourth amendment applied both to wiretapping and to electronic bugging, regardless of
physical trespass, thus requiring prior court approval for employment
of either device under a procedure which would satisfy the specificity
requirements of *Berger*.

In the Omnibus Crime Control and Safe Streets Act of 1968[50]
Congress amended the Communications Act of 1934[51] so that its pro-
hibition of interception and divulgence of communications is confined
to radio communications, and established a procedure for judicial
approval of wiretapping and electronic bugging that arguably does not
meet the requirements of the *Berger* case.[52] That act also contains the
following remarkable provision:

> Nothing contained in this chapter or in section 605 of the
> Communications Act of 1934 . . . shall limit the constitutional
> power of the President to take such measures as he deems
> necessary to protect the Nation . . . against foreign intelligence
> activities. . . . [or] limit the constitutional power of the Pres-
> ident to take such measures as he deems necessary to protect
> the United States against the overthrow of the Government by

---

45 N.Y. Times, June 21, 1969, at 11, col. 1.

46 *Hearings on Dep't of Justice Appropriations for 1971 Before a Subcomm. of the
House Comm. on Appropriations*, 91st Cong., 2d Sess., 754 (1970) [hereinafter cited as *1971
FBI Appropriations Hearings*].

47 388 U.S. 41 (1967).

48 The fourth amendment was held applicable to the states in Wolf v. Colorado, 388
U.S. 25 (1949), and to require the exclusion in state courts of products of an illegal search
in Mapp v. Ohio, 367 U.S. 643 (1961).

49 389 U.S. 347 (1967). Since these remarks were written, the use of the informer
wired for sound, earlier approved in On Lee v. United States, 343 U.S. 747 (1952), has
been resuscitated. United States v. White, 91 S.Ct. 1122 (1971).

50 18 U.S.C. §§ 2510-20 (Supp. V, 1970).

51 47 U.S.C. §§ 501, 605 (1964).

52 *See* Schwartz, *The Legitimation of Electronic Eavesdropping: The Politics of "Law
and Order,"* 67 MICH. L. REV. 455, 460-477 (1969).

force or other unlawful means, or against any other clear and present danger to the structure or existence of the Government.[53]

Whatever else this provision may do, it has emboldened Attorney General Mitchell to make the argument that the President has "inherent power . . . derived from the Constitution itself," free from judicial review under the fourth amendment, to employ wiretaps and electronic bugs "to gather foreign intelligence information" and "to gather intelligence information deemed necessary to protect the nation from attempts of domestic organizations to use unlawful means to attack and subvert the existing structure of the government."[54] This argument was first made and accepted by Judge Julius Hoffman in a case where the domestic threat to the "structure of the government" consisted of the disturbances at the Democratic National Convention in Chicago in 1968.[55] It has been rejected by the United States Court of Appeals for the Sixth Circuit and by a federal district court in California.[56]

B. The Compiling Federal Agencies

So much for sources.[57] What of the official dossiers compiled from these sources? Starting with the proposition that it is probably

---

[53] 18 U.S.C. § 2511(3) (Supp. V, 1970).

[54] Brief for United States at 9, United States v. Dellinger, No. 69CR180 (N.D. Ill., Feb. 20, 1970) (Chicago Conspiracy Trial).

[55] United States v. Dellinger, No. 69CR180 (N.D. Ill., Feb. 20, 1970). The government's argument as to foreign intelligence information was accepted in United States v. Brown, 317 F. Supp. 531 (E.D. La. 1970). *Cf.* United States v. Clay, 430 F.2d 165 (5th Cir. 1970), *cert. granted,* 91 S.Ct. 457 (1971); United States v. Stone, 305 F. Supp. 75 (D.D.C. 1969).

[56] United States v. Sinclair, 321 F. Supp. 1074 (E.D. Mich. 1971), *petition for mandamus denied sub nom.* United States v. United States Dist. Ct., Civ. No. 71-1105 (6th Cir., Apr. 8, 1971); United States v. Smith, 321 F. Supp. 424 (C.D. Cal. 1971). By separate concurring opinions in Katz v. United States, 389 U.S. 347 (1967), Justice White has approved and Justices Douglas and Black have rejected the notion that the government is not subject to judicial review under the fourth amendment in "national security" cases.

The Omnibus Crime Control and Safe Streets Act also requires annual reports to Congress of all court-approved wiretaps and bugs under the Act obtained by either federal or state authorities. 18 U.S.C. § 2519 (Supp. V, 1970). For the first full year of operation under the Act in 1969 these reports revealed 30 federal interceptions and 241 state interceptions, 176 of the latter being in New York alone. Ad. Office of United States Courts, Report on Applications for Orders Authorizing or Approving the Interception of Wire or Oral Communications, Table I (1969). For the second year there were court authorizations for 183 federal interceptions and 414 state interceptions, including 215 by New York and 132 by New Jersey. N.Y. Times, May 3, 1971, at 1, col. 4. But the federal figures do not reveal all federal wiretaps because the federal government is acting on Attorney General Mitchell's contention that no court approval is required for tapping and bugging in "national security" cases. On a single day in March 1970, the FBI alone had 36 wiretaps and 2 bugs operating in cases so classified. *1971 FBI Appropriations Hearings, supra* note 46, at 754.

[57] The governmental compilers also have another source of information not available to private compilers—the "mail cover" provided by the Post Office department. *See* 39

quite literally true that God only knows what is contained in the files of the CIA, some information is available about the files of some of the more obvious compilers.

1. FBI.—There has never been an official investigation of the FBI. Congressional committees occasionally hear something *about* the FBI, but, save J. Edgar Hoover's annual appearances before appropriations committees, Congress never hears *from* the FBI.[58] From Hoover's appearances we are advised that the FBI's computerized National Crime Information Center, which is tied to 24 computerized terminals throughout the country, contains in excess of 1.7 million personal files and contains also more than 195 million sets of fingerprints. The latter collection (with a substantial assist from state police forces and the Selective Service System and a lesser one from the tourists visiting the FBI headquarters who are persuaded to leave their fingerprints) is increasing at the rate of about 7 million per year.[59] Even with some allowance for foreigners, coverage must be approaching 100% of the adult population of the United States.

We can only speculate about the contents of the 1.7 million files. They are not disclosed to the public except as Hoover sees fit to reveal their contents in a book, an article or a speech.[60] But we can be sure that they are not confined to information related to enforcing the criminal laws. Since 1947 the FBI has been investigating federal em-

---

C.F.R. § 113.7 (1970). This source provides the name and address of the sender of mail to a suspect and, if desired, a facsimile of the sender's handwriting. *Hearings on Invasion of Privacy (Gov't Agencies) Before the Subcomm. on Ad. Practice & Procedure of the Senate Judiciary Comm.*, 89th Cong., 1st Sess., pt. 1, at 67, 117-120 (1965). The Post Office provides this service on request of any federal or state law enforcement agency, and averages about 1,000 mail covers per month. *Id.* at 68, 75, 83, 88, 93-94. One of the chief users of the service is the internal Revenue Service, but both it and the Post Office declined to supply Congressional investigators with the names of those subjected to such surveillance, not only because some were still under investigation but also because such disclosure would constitute an invasion of the privacy of those investigated and found innocent of tax violations! *Id.* at 78, 97, 216. Although not specifically authorized by statute, the Post Office finds authority for the practice in its general statutory power to prescribe rules and superintend the business of the department. *Id.* at 68; *see* 39 U.S.C. § 501 (1964). Furthermore, the practice survived a challenge that it violated provisions of the criminal code forbidding delay of the mails. United States v. Costello, 255 F.2d 876 (2d Cir. 1958), *cert. denied*, 357 U.S. 937 (1958). *See also*, United States v. Schwartz, 283 F.2d 107 (3rd Cir. 1960), *cert. denied*, 364 U.S. 942 (1961).

[58] The authors of private studies of the FBI, which are now numerically balanced for [H. OVERSTREET & B. OVERSTREET, THE FBI IN OUR OPEN SOCIETY (1969); D. WHITEHEAD, THE FBI STORY (1956)] and against [F. COOK, THE FBI NOBODY KNOWS (1964); M. LOWENTHAL, THE FEDERAL BUREAU OF INVESTIGATION (1950)], were able to learn little about FBI files.

[59] *1971 FBI Appropriations Hearings, supra* note 46, at 692, 694, 712, 714. The problems confronting one who seeks to compel the FBI to remove from its files his fingerprints and notations covering his arrest and release without charge by state police were suggested but not resolved in Menard v. Mitchell, 430 F.2d 486 (D.C. Cir. 1970).

[60] *See, e.g.,* J. HOOVER, J. EDGAR HOOVER ON COMMUNISM (1969); J. HOOVER, A STUDY OF COMMUNISM (1962); J. HOOVER, MASTERS OF DECEIT (1958).

ployees and applicants for federal employment under the Federal Loyalty-Security Program, and since that time the Program has expanded
to cover the employees of those who contract with various agencies and
departments of the government. Investigations under that program
delve even more deeply into the morality, beliefs and associations of
the subjects than do the investigations conducted for private employers
and insurance companies.[61]

If this were the extent of FBI surveillance, most of us who have
never worked for, or sought to work for, the executive branch of the
federal government or its contractors, and who have never done any-
thing which would be likely to make us suspects of a federal crime
(including the burgeoning list of political crimes), might be tempted
to rest easy. But that is not all. Under the Emergency Detention Act
of 1950[62] the President is authorized to declare an "Internal Security
Emergency" in the event of invasion, declaration of war or "[i]nsur-
rection within the United States in aid of a foreign enemy." In that
event, the Attorney General is to apprehend and incarcerate "each
person as to whom there is reasonable ground to believe that such
person will engage in, or probably will conspire with others to engage
in, acts of espionage or sabotage." Obviously, speed will be of the essence
and any diligent Attorney General charged with enforcing this Act
must have a list of suspects prepared in advance. Data supposed to support such a list is doubtless lodged in the files of the FBI.

The FBI has long operated under a Department of Justice order
providing:

> Except upon specific authorization of the Attorney Gen-
> eral, no officer or employee shall forward to any person out-
> side the Department of Justice . . . any information obtained
> from the Federal Bureau of Investigation . . . .[63]

But there are vaguely authorized exceptions. Department regulations

---

61 From a careful study of all available data, Professor Ralph Brown concluded in
1958 that the federal program then covered more than 13 million people, or one-fifth of
the national labor force. R. Brown, Loyalty and Security 181 (1958). The same fraction
today would produce a figure in excess of 16 million. U.S. Bureau of the Census, Statistical Abstract of the United States 213 (1970). Professor Brown also estimated that the
cumulative total of those dismissed under the program in 1958 was in excess of 10,000. R.
Brown, *supra*, at 182. It is a fair guess that their names, and the names of many others
who were not dismissed but about whom derogatory information was recorded, are
included in the FBI files. But there is no reason to suppose that all of them are included in
the 1.7 million files reported in the National Crime Information Center.

62 50 U.S.C. §§ 811-826 (1964).

63 Hoover, *The Confidential Nature of FBI Reports*, 8 Syracuse L. Rev. 2, 11 n.10
(1956). *See also* United States *ex rel.* Touhy v. Ragen, 340 U.S. 462 (1951). This order is
still in effect. Letter from Helen W. Gandy, Office of the Director, FBI, March 23, 1971.

allow for exchange of "identification records, including personal fingerprints voluntarily submitted," with "law enforcement and other governmental agencies" and the operation of "a central clearinghouse of police statistics . . . and a computerized nation-wide index of law enforcement information under the National Crime Information Center."[64] And "the FBI has long followed a policy, approved by several Attorneys General, of relaying information believed to be of interest to other Government agencies."[65] Moreover, although the official position of the FBI forbids disclosure of files to private parties, there is reason to doubt adherence in the field.[66]

2. *The Internal Revenue Service.*—Most adults in the country are required to initiate a file with the IRS by filing a tax return. The file is augmented when the IRS launches an investigation of tax liability or has to resort to collection efforts.

In 1965 the Commissioner of Internal Revenue admitted[67] to a Congressional committee that the Service had in the past used two-way mirrors and bugging devices in conference rooms where taxpayers and their lawyers met prior to and during discussions with IRS agents. The Commissioner further admitted that some agents, in an excess of "zeal emanating from the highest motives," had employed illegal bugs and wiretaps. He assured the committee that all such practices had been terminated.[68] Another practice, not disavowed by the IRS but now forbidden by Congress, involved the opening of a taxpayer's first class mail, either in search of evidence of tax liability or in search for assets from which taxes might be collected.[69]

---

64 28 C.F.R. § 0.85 (1970); *cf.* 28 U.S.C. § 534 (1964).

65 Hoover, *A Comment on the Article "Loyalty Among Government Employees,"* 58 YALE L.J. 401, 403 (1949).

66 Mayor Alioto of San Francisco recently told a Senate subcommittee that he had proof that the FBI had supplied information to *Look* magazine for an article charging him with underworld connections. N.Y. Times, March 4, 1971, at 22, col. 1. [This and all subsequent citations to newspaper reports of testimony refer to testimony in hearings currently being conducted by the Subcommittee on Constitutional Rights of the Senate Judiciary Committee.] The Department of Justice replied that an FBI agent had not "furnished," but had "confirmed," information which the magazine might have obtained from other federal agencies and that the agent involved had been disciplined and forced to retire. N.Y. Times, March 10, 1971, at 1, col. 6; Washington Post, March 10, 1971, at 1, col. 4.

67 *Hearings on Invasion of Privacy (Gov't Agencies) Before the Subcomm. on Ad. Practice & Procedure of the Senate Judiciary Comm.,* 89th Cong., 1st Sess., pt. 3, at 1130, 1133-1143 (1965).

68 Later the Commissioner advised the Committee that the agents engaging in illegal eavesdropping had been disciplined by reprimand and transferred and that there had been some voluntary separations from the service. *Hearings on S. 928 Before the Subcomm. on Ad. Practice & Procedure of the Senate Judiciary Comm.,* 90th Cong., 1st Sess., pt. 2, at 116 (1967). There was, of course, no mention of criminal prosecution.

69 Federal statutes forbid, and prescribe criminal penalties for, the opening of first class letters or parcels by anyone save an employee in the dead letter office or a person holding a search warrant. 18 U.S.C. § 1072 (1964); 39 U.S.C. § 4057 (1964). *See also* 39 C.F.R. § 117.1 (1970). But it is a nuisance to obtain a search warrant, the application for the warrant must make some showing of probable cause for the search, the warrant may be

It might be supposed that information that the government compels the citizen to supply in his tax returns would be held in confidence and used only for the purpose for which it is supplied. In fact, the confidentiality of tax returns is preserved by a statute that has all of the containing qualities of a sieve.[70] Tax returns are fully available to state tax officials,[71] to any Congressional committee "authorized to investigate returns," and to anyone authorized by Executive Order.[72]

3. The Armed Services.—The Army, of course, has personal files on those who are, or have been, in its service. In addition, as a former captain of Army intelligence recently revealed, the Army since 1965 has been collecting information on civilians in its computerized data bank at Fort Holabird in Baltimore, ostensibly to enable the Army to anticipate civil disturbances.[73] Subsequently, the Army assured a congressman that the surveillance of civilians would cease and that all

---

annoyingly specific about the items to be seized, and there have even been instances where warrants have been refused. Hence, the IRS hit upon a more "efficient" scheme.

Provisions of the Internal Revenue Code authorize the IRS to make its own administrative levy on "property of" a taxpayer "for the payment of" taxes. 26 U.S.C. § 6331 (1964), *as amended*, (Supp. V, 1970). These provisions also direct that "as soon as practicable after the seizure of the property" it shall be sold. 26 U.S.C. § 6335 (1964), *as amended*, (Supp. V, 1970). In any event, they reach only to property of the taxpayer, and postal regulations provide that the sender of mail may reclaim it at any time before it is delivered to the addressee. 39 C.F.R. § 153.5 (1970). Nonetheless, it was the practice of the IRS to serve levies on the Post Office and the practice of the Post Office to surrender undelivered mail addressed to taxpayers—not for the purpose of sale, but for the purpose of opening and examining by the IRS. *Hearings on Invasion of Privacy (Gov't Agencies) Before the Subcomm. on Ad. Practice & Procedure of the Senate Judiciary Comm.*, 89th Cong., 1st Sess., pt. 2, at 352-54, 360-61, 366-67, 369-71, 380-86 (1965). When this practice was exposed, Congress promptly amended the Internal Revenue Code to exempt all undelivered mail from the IRS levy. 26 U.S.C. § 6334(a)(5) (Supp. V, 1970).

[70] 26 U.S.C. § 6103 (1964), *as amended*, (Supp. V, 1970).

[71] It has been reported that at least 45 million of some 75 million returns filed in 1970 were put on computer tapes and mailed to at least 30 states. Wall St. J., April 21, 1970, at 1, col. 6.

[72] Between 1957 and 1970 53 such orders have been issued. Historical note to 26 U.S.C.A. § 6103 (1967 & Supp. 1971). These orders are not confined to the returns of named persons, but authorize inspections of all returns for designated periods of years. They have opened the federal tax returns to various federal agencies and Congressional committees not charged with tax responsibilities. Two of the chief beneficiaries of these Presidential dispensations have been two committees that have nothing to do with internal revenue matters. One is the House Internal Security Committee (neé House Un-American Activities Committee). *See, e.g.*, Exec. Order No. 11465, 3 C.F.R. § 116 (1969). The other is the Senate Subcommittee on Internal Security. *See, e.g.*, Exec. Order No. 11505, 35 Fed. Reg. 939 (1970).

Moreover, in relying on these Executive Orders, I am substantially understating the extent to which tax returns or their contents are disseminated. Disclosures about a year ago that Presidential aide Clark Mollenhoff was examining tax returns without an Executive Order—or at least without a published order—led to further disclosures that similar practices were followed in the Kennedy administration. It was reported also that IRS employees had not infrequently leaked the contents of returns to others and that in one instance a friendly revenue agent had obliged a federal prosecutor by screening the tax returns of 150 prospective jurors in a tax case. No one could recall, however, that any IRS employee had ever been prosecuted under a statute, *e.g.*, 26 U.S.C. § 7213 (1964), imposing criminal penalties for such activities. Wall St. J., April 21, 1970, at 1, col. 6; Wall St. J., April 27, 1970, at 8, col. 2.

[73] Pyle, *CONUS Intelligence: The Army Watches Civilian Politics*, WASH. MONTHLY, Jan. 1970, at 4; N.Y. Times, Jan. 16, 1970, at 26, col. 1.

dossiers would be destroyed.[74] Belying this assurance was a later announcement by Secretary Laird that surveillance operations had been transferred to civilian control in the Department of Defense.[75]

In hearings currently in process before a Senate subcommittee, Defense Department spokesmen revealed[76] that since 1968 the Department has maintained an index of 25 million names that includes both civilians who have taken part in civil rights or antiwar activities, and prominent persons[77] friendly with such suspects. In defense of this practice, the Army assured Congress that its share of the dossiers—about 8 million—was accessible to only 688 authorized officials.[78] In addition, Assistant Attorney General William Rehnquist conceded abuses due to "excessive zeal," and testified that the surveillance of civilians has now been transferred from Defense to Justice. However, he opposed any legislative limitations on such surveillance and urged the Congress to rely upon the "self-discipline" of the executive branch.[79]

4. The House Internal Security Committee.—Not all the dossier compilers in the federal government are in the executive branch. Since 1938 the House Un-American Activities Committee (rechristened the House Internal Security Committee in 1969) has been compiling dossiers on persons and organizations not sufficiently anti-Communist to suit its tastes. (In a much more sporadic fashion, the Senate Internal Security Subcommittee has done the same thing.) Although the Supreme Court has ruled[80] that the Committee's procedures do not include minimum safeguards to insure the rationality of its compilations, these compilations are, nonetheless, widely used and easily available. Anyone can obtain a copy of a Committee dossier merely by having it requested by a member of Congress.[81]

---

[74] N.Y. Times, March 13, 1970, at 26, col. 6.

[75] N.Y. Times, Dec. 24, 1970, at 1, col. 2.

[76] *See* remarks of Senator Birch Bayh, 117 CONG. REC. S. 2290 (daily ed. March 2, 1971); N.Y. Times, Feb. 26, 1971, at 8, col. 3; Boston Globe, Feb. 28, 1971, at 31, col. 1.

[77] The list includes Senator Adlai Stevenson III, Representative Abner Mikva, and former Illinois Governor Otto Kerner. N.Y. Times, Feb. 13, 1971, at 31, col. 1.

[78] Washington Post, March 3, 1971, at 1, col. 2.

[79] N.Y. Times, March 10, 1971, at 1, col. 6; Washington Post, March 10, 1971, at 1, col. 4.

Before the Congressional hearings started, the ACLU had filed two actions to enjoin the Army's civilian surveillance programs as a violation of the first and fourth amendments and of a constitutionally protected right of privacy. In each instance the complaint was dismissed, and in both cases appeals were taken. In one of the cases the Court of Appeals for the District of Columbia reversed and ordered the Army to trial. Tatum v. Laird, No. 24203 (D.C. Cir., Apr. 27, 1971); ACLU v. Westmoreland, 39 U.S.L.W. 2401 (N.D. Ill., Jan 5, 1971).

[80] Dombrowski v. Pfister, 380 U.S. 479, 496 (1965).

[81] During the past year the Committee responded to over 1000 such requests, and its files were also examined by 25 executive departments and agencies of the federal government. H.R. REP. No. 92-14, 91st Cong., 2d Sess., 166 (1970). In 1968 Congressman Don Edwards wrote to several executive agencies and departments and asked them to what extent they searched Committee files and why. All responded that they searched the files

The Committee publishes a cumulative index that includes the names of all individuals, organizations and publications mentioned in any of the various publications of the Committee. An index for the period 1938-54 included some 38,000 names of individuals;[82] a supplement published last year lists about 25,000 names mentioned between 1955 and 1968 in Committee reports, hearings or "consultations."[83] Of course one has no grounds to protest inclusion in a list which includes, among others, all known and suspected members of the Communist party and the Ku Klux Klan, since the Committee declares (in fine print) in the front of the index:

> The fact that a name appears in this index simply indicates that said individual, publication or organization has been mentioned in a hearing, report, or consultation. It is not per se an indication of a record of subversive activities. A careful check of references in the hearing, report, or consultation will determine the circumstances under which such individual, publication or organization is named.[84]

Anyone who has the time and access to the Committee's many hearings and reports can check out the basis for including most of the names in the listing. The Committee does not explain, however, how one is

in connection with the federal loyalty-security program and estimated the frequency of their searches as follows: Housing and Urban Development Dep't, "[A]bout once a month"; Health, Education and Welfare Dep't, "[S]everal times each week"; Defense Dep't, "[A]pproximately 120 times a week"; Civil Service Comm'n, "[A]pproximately 288,000 times in fiscal 1967." 114 CONG. REC. 6271-6272 (1968).

Congressman Edward Koch has recently introduced a bill, applicable only to the House Internal Security Committee, which would require the Committee to notify each individual on which it keeps a file, to allow the individual to inspect and supplement the file (but not learn the source of information in it), and to forbid any disclosure of the file outside the Committee and its staff without the consent of the subject—but with a blanket exception from all these provisions for files that two-thirds of the Committee decide should "be kept secret in the interest of national security." H.R. 841, 92d Cong., 1st Sess. (1971).

Last summer the Committee sent a questionnaire to 179 colleges and universities asking them to list all campus speakers for the previous two year period, together with the honoraria paid. By matching the replies received with its dossiers on those named, the Committee produced and released to the press a list of 65 "radical" campus speakers. N.Y. Times, Oct. 15, 1970, at 23, col. 3. Some of these listed protested and the list was pared down to 57.

The American Civil Liberties Union brought an action to enjoin official publication and distribution of the list. Judge Gesell decided that he could not direct an injunction to Committee members because of the speech or debate clause, U.S. CONST. art. I, § 6, cl. 1, but the court did enjoin the Public Printer from printing or distributing the list, which he found to have no legitimate legislative purpose, but to be designed solely to appeal to college officials, alumni and parents in an effort to inhibit free speech on the campuses. Hentoff v. Ichord, 318 F. Supp. 1175 (D.D.C. 1970). Although the government has appealed the decision, the Committee persuaded the House to adopt a resolution directing the Printer to publish the list and he has done so. *See* 116 CONG. REC. H. 11606-25 (daily ed. Dec. 14, 1970); H.R. REP. No. 91-1732, 91st Cong., 2d Sess. 7 (1970).

[82] CUMULATIVE INDEX TO PUBLICATIONS OF THE COMM. ON UN-AMERICAN ACTIVITIES 1938-54, at 15-961 (1962).

[83] SUPPLEMENT TO CUMULATIVE INDEX TO PUBLICATIONS OF THE COMM. ON UN-AMERICAN ACTIVITIES 1955-68, at 19-587 (1970).

[84] *Id.* at 1.

to check out its "consultations." Presumably one asks his Congressman to obtain a copy of the Committee's dossier on the subject.

   5. *The Census Bureau.*—Although the Constitution directs a decennial "enumeration" of the population for the purposes of apportioning representatives among the states,[85] the Department of Commerce through the Census Bureau is now directed by statute to collect and publish information not only on the population but also on industry, business, agriculture, governments, on crime and on defective, dependent and delinquent classes.[86] The population census, far from being a mere "enumeration," now covers matters of sex, race, national origin, place of birth, marital status, family size, nature of household, quality of housing, geographical location, and mobility.[87] In addition to information collected for itself, the Census Bureau also obtains information from other agencies, such as the Internal Revenue Service and the Social Security Administration.[88] Like the benevolent private compilers, the Census Bureau is interested not in individuals, but in groups. But, as with private compilers, the Bureau's compilations cannot be kept up to date or programmed for new uses unless a key to the identity of each individual is preserved.

   The law requires everyone over the age of eighteen to respond to the Bureau's inquiries.[89] The Bureau is authorized to furnish state governments, courts, and individuals with "data for genealogical and other proper purposes" although the information so furnished is not to be "used to the detriment of" the subject.[90] The Bureau is forbidden to use the information for "other than . . . statistical purposes" or to permit anyone outside the Department of Commerce to "examine . . . individual reports"[91] and criminal penalties are prescribed for unauthorized disclosure of information.[92]

---

   [85] U.S. CONST., art. I, § 2, cl. 3.
   [86] 13 U.S.C. §§ 101-61 (1964).
   [87] Not all 200 million of us answer all questions. In the 1970 census, 80% received a short form questionnaire covering age, race, marital status and housing. Fifteen percent received a longer form and 5% received the longest form. N.Y. Times, April 1, 1970, at 47, col. 4. A citizen's attempt to compel the Bureau to frame inquiries that would lay the basis for reduction in the Congressional representation pursuant to § 2 of the fourteenth amendment for states discriminating against voters on the basis of race ended in dismissal of his complaint in Lampkin v. Connor, 360 F.2d 505 (D.C. Cir. 1966). *See also* Prieto v. Stans, 321 F. Supp. 420 (N.D. Cal. 1970).
   [88] *Hearings on 1970 Census Questions Before the House Comm. on Post Office and Civil Service,* 89th Cong., 2d Sess. 28 (1966).
   [89] 13 U.S.C. § 221 (1964). *See* United States v. Sharrow, 309 F.2d 77 (2d Cir. 1962), *cert. denied,* 372 U.S. 949 (1963). The fourth amendment offers no protection. United States v. Rickenbacker, 309 F.2d 462 (2d Cir. 1962), *cert. denied,* 371 U.S. 962 (1963).
   [90] 13 U.S.C. § 8 (1964).
   [91] 13 U.S.C. § 9(a) (1964).
   [92] 13 U.S.C. § 214 (1964).

The Bureau claims that there has never been a known violation of these restrictions on use and that it does not supply individual information to other federal agencies.[93] But the Federal Trade Commission found a loophole. Pursuant to an investigation of possible violation of antitrust laws, it issued an administrative subpoena for a corporation's file copy of its census returns. The Supreme Court, in an opinion equally applicable to all census returns and probably to tax returns as well, held that the subpoena should be judicially enforced although the "confidential" census report form stated that it could not "be used for purposes of taxation, investigation or regulation." Both the legend on the forms and the statutory restrictions on disclosure were held to run only against the Census Bureau and not to impose limitations on the power of other governmental agencies to compel the subject to disclose its file copies.[94] Congress promptly amended the law to forbid any governmental agency to obtain copies of census returns retained by the subject.[95]

This survey of official dossier compilers is by no means complete, even at the federal level. For instance, an Associated Press study last year reported that the Civil Service Commission has files on 10 million persons who have sought federal jobs since 1939 and additional files on 1.5 million suspected of "subversive activities," all of whom presumably have lost or will never obtain federal employment. The Secret Service also has computerized 100,000 names and accumulated 50,000 dossiers.[96] Personal files are also kept on virtually all of the labor force by the Social Security Administration and the Passport Office keeps a computerized file of more than 243,000 citizens whose applications for passports are to be brought to the attention of law enforcement agencies.[97] A 1966 survey of all federal executive departments and agencies revealed that they had 3.1 billion personal files, including 264.6 million police records, 342 million medical histories, 279.6 million psychiatric records and 187.8 million "security or other investigative reports."[98]

Congressman Edward Koch and Senator Birch Bayh have intro-

---

[93] *Hearings on 1970 Census Questions Before the House Comm. on Post Office and Civil Service,* 89th Cong., 2d Sess. 27-28 (1966).

[94] St. Regis Paper Co. v. United States, 368 U.S. 208 (1961).

[95] 13 U.S.C. § 9 (1964).

[96] Boston Herald-Traveler, April 19, 1970, at 43, col. 1.

[97] N.Y. Times, Feb. 11, 1971, at 11, col. 1.

[98] SENATE SUBCOMM. ON AD. PRACTICE & PROCEDURE, GOV'T DOSSIER (SURVEY OF INFORMATION CONTAINED IN GOV'T FILES) 90th Cong., 1st Sess., 19, 26-27 (Comm. Print 1967). *See also The Computerization of Government Files: What Impact on the Individual?,* 15 U.C.L.A.L. REV. 1371 (1968); S. WHEELER, ON RECORD (1969).

duced bills[99] to enact a Citizen's Privacy Act. Applicable to all federal agencies and departments subject to the Administrative Procedure Act—but not to Congressional committees—the Act would impose the same requirements of notice to the subject and opportunity to supplement the file and nondisclosure without the subject's consent as Representative Koch's bill would impose on the House Internal Security Committee[100]—but with exceptions for files "compiled for law enforcement purposes" so long as "reasonably necessary to commence prosecution or other action" and for files "specifically required by Executive order to be kept secret in the interest of the national security."

III. TOWARD A NATIONAL DATA BANK: DANGERS AND INADEQUATE SAFEGUARDS

As previously indicated, there was a proposal a few years ago, originating with certain academics and encouraged by the Bureau of the Budget, to establish a Federal Data Center, not for the purpose of compiling personal dossiers, but solely to compile statistical information on groups. During Congressional hearings it was conceded that some

---

99 H.R. 854 & S. 975, 92d Cong., 1st Sess. (1971).

100 See note 81 supra.

What the federal government is doing in this area, the states are doing also. The New York State Identification and Intelligence System, established in 1965, has a computerized central data bank serving 3,600 law enforcement agencies in the state. N.Y. Times, March 11, 1971, at 26, col. 4. The Oklahoma Office of Inter-Agency Coordination, established in 1969 with Federal Law Enforcement Assistance funds, is now facing an ACLU lawsuit seeking the dismantling of 6,000 dossiers. Civil Liberties, February, 1971, at 1, col. 3; Civil Liberties, October, 1970, at 1, col. 1. The Massachusetts Civil Liberties Union is preparing a similar suit against the State Police's Subversive Activities Division, whose continued operation is also being challenged in the state legislature. The Docket, February, 1971, at 1, col. 3. In a New Orleans suit now before the Fifth Circuit the commander of the city's intelligence division has testified that his men attend and take photographs at all public events at which "controversial" views are likely to be expressed. Civil Liberties, July, 1970, at 2, col. 1. In New Jersey, the Attorney General sent a memorandum to all local law enforcement officials asking them to report to the State Police Central Security Unit the names of all persons involved in "incidents" such as "civil disturbance, riot, rally, protest, demonstration, march, confrontation, etc.," including information on spouses, draft status, affiliations, education and credit status. In a class action for a declaratory judgment that such a program violated the first amendment, the trial court gave summary judgment for the plaintiffs and ordered the Attorney General to produce and destroy all dossiers except when they "will be used to charge persons with specifically defined criminal conduct." Anderson v. Sills, 106 N.J. Super. 545, 256 A.2d 298 (Ch. 1969). On appeal, the decision was reversed and remanded. The summary judgment was held improper because the supreme court seemed to view as fanciful plaintiff's fears that the dossiers would be improperly used. Anderson v. Sills, 56 N.J. 210, 265 A.2d 678 (1970) (an amended complaint has been filed in the case). For discussion of the trial court decision, see Askin, Police Dossiers and Emerging Principles of First Amendment Adjudication, 22 STAN. L. REV. 196 (1970). See also Comment, Secret Files: Legitimate Police Activity or Unconstitutional Restraint on Dissent?, 58 GEO. L.J. 569 (1970); Note, Chilling Political Expression by Use of Police Intelligence Files, 5 HARV. CIV. RIGHTS-CIV. LIB. L. REV. 79 (1970).

key to the identity of those in the group must be maintained if the group compilations were to be kept current and remain adaptable to new uses.[101] In consequence a commitment was obtained from the Bureau of the Budget that before such a central data bank would be established, the problems of threat to privacy would be first evaluated by a panel of constitutional lawyers, computer experts, suppliers and users of statistical information, and representatives of Congress.[102] Although no further action has been taken, one should not conclude that the issue of a National Data Bank is an issue for another day. The vast numbers of personal dossiers already assembled by private and official compilers have effectively created a "National Data Bank" now. While a truly centralized National Data Bank might be more efficient, the present system is more vulnerable to unauthorized use and abuse.

Computerization by both private and governmental compilers is rapidly facilitating the advent of a national, centralized system. Many noncomputerized compilers are either in the process of computerizing or are feeding their dossiers into the computers of other compilers. The federal government, which acquired its first all-electronic computer during World War II, was using over 2000 computers by 1964.[103]

The computer can store infinite bits of information and can retrieve them within a few billionths of a second.[104] Computers can be connected by interfaces and can be tapped, not only by theft of printouts or by wires, but also by laser beams and other non-mechanical intrusions. Access codes can be and are broken, after which the intruder can "display and manipulate the data stored within the system."[105] No completely effective security system against such intrusions has been or probably ever will be devised.[106]

The intruder seeking data about a particular individual needs to locate a key to the pertinent data, but this task in many cases may not pose much difficulty. Enough advance knowledge about the subject to pose a few pertinent questions to the raided computer will quickly

101 *See* hearings cited in note 33 *supra*.

102 H.R. REP. No. 1842, 90th Cong., 2d Sess. 22-23 (1968).

103 H.R. REP. No. 802, 89th Cong., 1st Sess. 6 (1965); HOUSE COMM. ON POST OFFICE AND CIVIL SERVICE, 1964 INVENTORY OF AUTOMATIC DATA PROCESSING (ADP) EQUIPMENT IN THE FEDERAL GOVERNMENT, 88th Cong., 2d Sess. 3, 10c (1964).

104 Miller, *Personal Privacy in the Computer Age*, 67 MICH. L. REV. 1091, 1095 (1969). Since these remarks were written Professor Arthur Miller has also published his valuable book, THE ASSAULT ON PRIVACY (1971).

105 Miller, *supra* note 104, at 1111, 1190; A. WESTIN, PRIVACY AND FREEDOM 79-80 (1967).

106 Testimony of Robert P. Henderson, Vice-President, Honeywell Information Systems, before Subcomm. on Constitutional Rights of Senate Judiciary Comm., 92d Cong., 1st Sess. (1971).

identify the subject. In other cases, an even easier key may be available: social security numbers.[107]

Computers not engaged in compiling dossiers or in tapping those that are can also make their contributions to the data bank. The airlines' computerized reservation service will reveal where you flew, whether you reserved a rental automobile for use there, and, perhaps, where you made hotel reservations. The hotels' computerized reservation service will reveal the latter information if the airlines' service does not, and will reveal also whether you shared the accomodation with one claimed to be your spouse. Your bank's computerized check processing system will reveal details of many of your expenditures and, as we move on to the checkless, cashless society, will ultimately reveal the details of your every expenditure.

Against this monstrous technological capacity to search out most of the details of our lives, the present state of the law and of most proposals for new law seem both inadequate to achieve their professed objectives and inadequate in the protection afforded even if those objectives could be achieved.

A. Insuring the Accuracy of Dossiers

Concern about the accuracy of the dossiers reflects what the computermen identify as the GIGO principle—Garbage In, Garbage Out. In fact, the computerization of personal dossiers may reflect the first literal application of that principle. Those investigating the personal characteristics of individuals have been known to comb through the subjects' garbage for clues.

The main thrust of the Fair Credit Reporting Act,[108] and of the proposals for legislative restrictions on some federal compilers,[109] is to attempt to insure that the information in our dossiers will be accurate. The chief mechanism to achieve this end contemplates notice to the subject with an opportunity for him to correct erroneous entries. These measures almost surely will not achieve their objectives for at least two reasons:

1. Failure to Receive Notice.—Many subjects will never receive notice of their dossiers. The only sanctions in the Fair Credit Re-

---

107 Social security numbers are entered on federal and many state tax returns. In many states the number is also one's drivers license number. One and a half billion of those 3.1 billion federal personal files also contain the subject's social security number. Senate Subcomm. on Ad. Practice & Procedure, Gov't Dossier (Survey of Information Contained in Gov't Files), 90th Cong., 1st Sess. 26 (Comm. Print 1967).

108 84 Stat. 1114, tit. VI (1970 U.S. Code Cong. & Ad. News 5142); see note 30 supra.

109 See note 81 & text accompanying notes 99, 100 supra.

porting Act are compensatory damages for negligent failure to give notice and punitive damages for wilful failure to give notice. Since the subjects who do not receive a notice will never know that they have a cause of action, there is a considerable incentive for compilers to be sparing with the notices.

The incentive to give notice is even less for compilers who are not excepted in "law enforcement" and "national security" cases under the proposed legislation applicable to executive departments and agencies, since the proposed law contains no sanctions of its own. It seems highly doubtful that the nebulous provisions of the Federal Tort Claims Act can be read to incorporate the compensatory damage provisions of the Fair Credit Reporting Act for failure to give notice.[110] Beyond this, there appears to be only the possibility of a mandamus action to compel compliance;[111] but this possibility is of little value to one who is unaware that he is the subject of a dossier. The proposed legislation applicable to the House Internal Security Committee also contains no sanctions of its own and seems even more toothless. The Federal Tort Claims Act extends only to executive departments and agencies;[112] a mandamus action may not reach members of Congress[113] and apparently will not reach Committee employees if the Committee is careful not to delegate to them the duty of giving notice.[114]

2. Inadequacy of the Remedy.—The credit reporting agencies succeeded in selling Congress the monstrous proposition that they should remain free to collect and disseminate erroneous dossiers— subject only to liability for malice or wilful intent to injure—and that the burden should fall upon their subjects to come forward and correct errors. The pending bills applicable to some federal compilers proceed on a similar assumption. But many subjects, even if they do receive notice, may conclude that life is too short, or their resources too limited, to make an effort toward correction. Particularly may they

---

[110] Liability is imposed on the United States for compensatory but not punitive damages for negligent or wrongful acts or omissions of officers and employees of executive departments and agencies "under circumstances where the United States, if a private person, would be liable to the claimant in accordance with the law of the place where the act or omission occurred" [28 U.S.C. § 1346(b) (1964)], and for damages "in the same manner and to the same extent as a private individual under like circumstances," 28 U.S.C. § 2674 (1964). In any event the liability does not extend to "an act or omission of an employee of the Government, exercising due care, in the execution of a statute or regulation . . ." 28 U.S.C. § 2680 (1964).

[111] 28 U.S.C. § 1361 (1964) gives the federal district courts original jurisdiction "of any action in the nature of mandamus to compel an officer or employee of the United States or any agency thereof to perform a duty owed to the plaintiff."

[112] 28 U.S.C. § 2671 (1964).

[113] *See* Hentoff v. Ichord, 318 F. Supp. 1175 (D.D.C. 1970).

[114] *See* note 110 *supra*.

reach this conclusion when they discover that they can neither learn the sources of adverse entries (except for credit bureau reports), nor compel deletion of such entries, but must content themselves with entering their version of matters in the file.

B. Restricting Access to Dossiers

The Fair Credit Reporting Act imposes two types of restrictions on access to the dossiers of commercial compilers without the consent of the subject. First, the compiler may furnish information only to persons and governmental agencies whom the compiler "has reason to believe" have a "legitimate business need" for the information. Any compiler that is negligent in determining its "reason to believe" is liable for compensatory damages, and any compiler that wilfully acts without such "reason to believe" may be liable for punitive damages. These remedies will doubtless be invoked almost as rarely as the criminal penalties prescribed for any compiler who knowingly and wilfully discloses information to an unauthorized individual. The standard for authorized access—"legitimate business need"—is very possibly too vague to satisfy due process requirements for a criminal statute and is certainly too vague to hold out much promise for an effective civil remedy.

Second, the Fair Credit Reporting Act forbids disclosure of more than identifying information concerning name, address and employment to any government agency that does not have a "legitimate business need"—except in response to court order. The restriction imposes no substantive limit upon governmental agencies empowered to issue subpoenas enforceable by court order though it does impose the procedural inconvenience of obtaining a court order.[115] This does not include the FBI, which has no subpoena power. Instead the FBI is left with three alternatives: first, it can stop using the files of the commercial compilers; second, its agents can obtain access to the files by means of false pretenses and risk prosecution by the Department of Justice; or third, its agents can without false pretenses persuade the commercial compilers to risk prosecution by the Department of Justice by knowingly and wilfully making an unauthorized disclosure. The record of Department of Justice prosecutions for illegal wiretaps under the Communications Act of 1934 strongly suggests that the FBI will not feel confined to the first alternative.

The Fair Credit Reporting Act also authorizes disclosure of dos-

---

115 See note 22 supra.

siers pursuant to "the written instructions of" the subject. But obviously, when the subject is seeking employment, insurance or even credit this consent in many cases will be far from voluntary.[116] Similarly, the proposed legislation applicable to some federal compilers would—with generous exceptions for "national security" and "law enforcement" files—forbid disclosure of information without the "permission" of the subject. Here again, any consent given by a subject seeking federal employment will often not be voluntary. In any instance, the limited sanctions available under these proposals are likely neither to deter improper disclosure, nor to provide effective relief to one injured by disclosure.

C. Limiting the Contents of Dossiers

There have been suggestions that limitations be placed upon the content of personal dossiers. Some proponents of a formal National Data Center, for instance, suggested that its files include only "statistical" data and not the personalized data found in FBI, IRS, military, civil service and medical records.[117] But these proponents came up with no standard precise enough to permit effective control. Moreover, they apparently contemplated the continued compilation of dossiers that would not be included in the National Data Center, and it is the existence of these dossiers combined with the ubiquitous computer that provides the present, informal, National Data Center. One proposed version of the Fair Credit Reporting Act sought to forbid commercial compilers from reporting "information which is not reasonably relevant for the purpose for which it is sought or which constitutes an undue infringement of the individual's right of privacy."[118] The compilers were able to persuade Congressmen that this restriction was intolerably vague.

With the present state of knowledge about the contents and the uses of dossiers, it seems unlikely that we can effectively define either the "legitimacy" of the "need" permitting access, or what information is "relevant" to that need. Even less can we define the balance to be struck between the "need" and a desirable preservation of privacy.

---

[116] Indeed, one of the compilers' arguments against compelling them to give the subject a copy of his dossier was that someone else might, by economic coercion, "invade his privacy" by compelling him to produce it. *Senate Credit Bureau Hearings I, supra* note 1, at 65; *Senate Credit Bureau Hearings II, supra* note 1, at 226.

[117] *See* Note, *Privacy and Efficient Government: Proposals for a National Data Center,* 82 HARV. L. REV. 400, 413-414 (1968).

[118] H.R. 16340, 91st Cong., 2d Sess. § 54 (1970).

IV. BUT WHAT ABOUT PRIVACY?

Even if all dossiers were absolutely accurate, or if remedies for inaccuracy were completely adequate, the question of the right to privacy would remain. By a "right to privacy" I do not mean to confine myself to the right to protection against unwanted publicity and palpable intrusion into private affairs that finds limited protection in some jurisdictions.[119] Nor do I confine myself to those recently emerging constitutional concepts that thus far have forged only slightly beyond the fourth amendment to permit married persons to receive birth control information,[120] or to allow individuals to contemplate obscene material in the sanctity of their own homes.[121]

I refer instead to a concept of privacy confined neither to protection against publicity nor to palpable intrusions, to a concept that Justice Brandeis described as "the right to be let alone—the most comprehensive of rights and the right most valued by civilized men."[122] Justice Douglas has characterized this concept as the freedom of the individual "to select for himself the time and circumstances when he will share his secrets with others and decide the extent of that sharing."[123] As others have said, "the essence of privacy is no more, and certainly no less, than the freedom of the individual to pick and choose for himself the time and circumstances under which, and most importantly, the extent to which, his attitudes, beliefs, behavior and opinions are to be shared with or withheld from others."[124] Such a concept of privacy is offended by the gross compilation of personal details, however accurately and delicately the dossier be compiled, and by the dissemination of those details whether to private or public users of the information and regardless of their number.

It seems inconceivable that courts or state legislatures, either by developing legal remedies or expanding constitutional safeguards, will establish this concept of privacy in time to meet the dangers of the computerized dossier. Only the Congress seems capable of acting with the requisite speed. And, in order for it to act effectively, it must first come to comprehend the concept of privacy that its efforts must be de-

---

119 *See* text accompanying notes 25-28 *supra.*
120 Griswold v. Connecticut, 381 U.S. 479 (1965).
121 Stanley v. Georgia, 394 U.S. 479 (1965). This decision is already suffering some erosion. *See* United States v. Thirty-Seven Photographs, 39 U.S.L.W. 4518 (U.S. May 3, 1971); United States v. Reidel, 39 U.S.L.W. 4523 (U.S. May 3, 1971).
122 Olmstead v. United States, 277 U.S. 438, 478 (1928) (dissenting opinion).
123 Warden v. Hayden, 387 U.S. 294, 323 (1967) (dissenting opinion).
124 Ruebhausen & Brim, *Privacy and Behavioral Research,* 65 COLUM. L. REV. 1184, 1189 (1965).

signed to insure. It must also rid itself of three misconceptions which it shares with many outside the Congress:

1. The misconception that whatever technology can produce should be used, although technology produces not because of need, but because production is possible.
2. The misconception that anyone who can show that information is useful, or comforting, to him in the conduct of private or public affairs has shown a "legitimate need" for its use.
3. The misconception that whatever is efficient is desirable.

If a meaningful concept of privacy be adopted and these three misconceptions be discarded, Congress could then approach the problem on the assumption that so long as dossiers exist on the present scale they will be used in disregard of whatever restrictions may be imposed on their use. Law enforcement officials "in an excess of zeal" will disregard those restrictions and, in an excess of tolerance, will not invoke criminal sanctions against themselves or others who similarly disregard those restrictions. And with the use of dossiers in its present magnitude, any privately enforceable remedies will not suffice to check unauthorized use.

The only hope for substantial protection of privacy against the computerized dossiers, therefore, is that they not exist—at least that they not exist on the present scale. And if the "legitimate need" for the dossiers were appraised as an actual need for a vital public purpose, rather than as a convenience or a comfort for any acceptable purpose, the great bulk of existing dossiers could be eliminated and the growth of dossiers in the future drastically curtailed. Careful study of the contents of various compilations, and careful consideration of the justification therefor, would be required before lines could be drawn. But it seems apparent that a rigorous application of the test of actual need for a vital public purpose would drastically clear the files.

To cite but a few examples: No such need justifies the retention in FBI files of all information amassed by it on all persons investigated in connection with a particular crime after the case has been closed. Similarly, there is no need to retain in both FBI and Civil Service Commission files the collection of gossip, rumor and hearsay—or even of hard facts—on an applicant for federal employment after his application has been denied. The only possible need for preserving keys to personal identity in the Census Bureau's population statistics is to facilitate keeping statistics current and adapting them to new

uses during the ten-year period between censuses. But is that need so
vital, and could it not perhaps be met instead by taking a population
census at more frequent intervals?

There is no need at all for the highly untrustworthy files of the
House Internal Security Committee. There is even room to doubt the
need for those permanent dossiers that constitute the life-blood of the
credit bureaus. As previously indicated, they are as likely to induce as
to preclude unwise credit extension. Yet the business volume of the
users of dossiers is so high that their losses are almost infinitesimal.[125]
If credit bureau customers can do this well on the unreliable information they now receive, how much worse would they if left to their
own devices? It is often assumed that without credit bureau dossiers
losses would greatly increase, with a concomitant increase in the cost
of consumer credit and a throttling of the economy based on that
credit. However, this mere assumption has not been explored sufficiently to justify perpetuation of credit bureau dossier compilation.

A rigorous inquiry into the actual need for existing compilations
would doubtless produce even louder incantations from compilers
about efficiency. It is more efficient to preserve dossiers for future
possible use than to require a new investigation of the subject whenever
information about him becomes necessary, or helpful, or comforting.
Certainly it is more efficient. But it is also more efficient to provide an
accessible file of every police investigation of anyone ever made, no matter how unwarranted, against the possibility that another investigation
may be made in the future. It is also more efficient for the Selective Service to provide the FBI with fingerprints and other data on all
persons it processes against the possibility that a small percentage of
them may be future law violators. It would also be more efficient to
extend the Alien Registration Act[126] to civilians. But we have not, in
this country, permitted efficiency to be the determining factor when
individual liberty is jeopardized. Instead, we have opted against efficiency and in favor of constitutional guarantees against unlawful
searches and seizures and self-incrimination and for jury trials in

---

125 I have asked many bankers and finance company representatives about their loss
ratios on consumer receivables and have yet to be given a figure higher than 0.5%. In
other instances the consumer finance companies have claimed a loss ratio of 1.5%. See
J. CHAPMAN & R. SHAY, THE CONSUMER FINANCE INDUSTRY 24 (1967). The bankers have
claimed 2%. P. McCRACKEN, J. MAO & C. FRICKE, CONSUMER INSTALLMENT CREDIT AND PUBLIC
POLICY 116 (1965). But the latest word I have seen, from a spokesman for the American
Bankers Association, is that on consumer transactions "in commercial banks the loss ratio
is less than half a percent; it is perhaps now getting close to a quarter of 1 percent."
Senate Credit Bureau Hearings II, supra note 1, at 322.
126 8 U.S.C. §§ 1301-1306 (1964).

criminal cases. In view of the massive threat to individual privacy posed by the present and growing body of computerized dossiers, efficiency will hardly serve as a justification for their preservation.

These are the assumptions on which Congressional inquiry should proceed. Recognizing these assumptions, Congress would doubtless conclude that most of our present National Data Bank must be wiped out, and that preservation of and access to the surviving dossiers must be restricted to an actual need to further a vital public purpose. Finally, mindful of these assumptions, Congress would not vest the policing of restrictions in the hands of the most probable violators.

We have not yet had an inquiry based on such assumptions. The time for that inquiry is overdue. The computerized dossiers are multiplying by the day. And we are only thirteen years from 1984.

Let's Everybody Litigate?

MAURICE ROSENBERG

I. Court Reform in Macro-Context: Managing Legal Conflict

In an era of rising assertiveness and multiplying pressures upon courts from the volume and heat of legal controversies, court system reformers must turn to new possibilities.[1] The experience of the generation just past teaches unmistakably that well-advertised specific cures for ailing courts have a consistent record of not working. Court problems are complicated, and measures that work well in one city fail in others. Steps that seem to perform magically when first tried soon become stale and ineffective, even in the same courthouse.

The great need is not a set of remedies for yesterday's—or even today's—maladies in the administration of justice. Court reformers must devise structures, procedures, and methods that take account of the inevitability of change; that not only will be ready for the problems

MAURICE ROSENBERG, professor of law, Columbia University. Maurice Rosenberg holds an A.B. from Syracuse University (1940), and an LL.B. from Columbia University (1947), where he also served as editor-in-chief of the *Columbia Law Review*. He was in private practice in New York City from 1949 to 1956, when he became an associate professor of law at Columbia University. Since 1958 he has been the Nash Professor of Law at Columbia. He has been visiting professor of law and social research at Harvard (1969–1970) and has served as a member of the (New York City) Mayor's Committee on the Judiciary since 1961. His publications include *Elements of Civil Procedure* (with Weinstein and Smit, 2d ed., 1970), *Cases and Materials on Conflict of Laws* (with Reese, 6th ed., 1971), *The Pretrial Conference and Effective Justice* (1964), and *Dollars, Delay and the Automobile Victim* (ed., 1968).

confronting courts on that day several years from now when the re-tooled system comes into being, but with luck will continue to respond for five, ten, or twenty years afterward.

Court system reformers must not confine themselves to asking how more cases can be pushed through the courts faster, or even to solving the question of how money for more courts, judges, and supporting personnel can be wrung from erratically thrifty legislatures. The challenge goes deeper.

Not only are more people constantly litigating more frequently with more intensity about more issues of familiar kinds, but Americans have also increasingly been defining as legal problems more and more forms of the distresses, anxieties, and wounds they once regarded as the slings and arrows of outrageous fortune, or as the responsibility of institutions other than the courts.

Today, a heightened sense of legal entitlements and expansive ideas about what judges can and will do are changing the society in dramatic ways, and largely through the courts. Whether this is good or ill, it is a factor the architects of court reform must have clearly in mind. Evaluating the options requires hard thinking about what courts are for, what they do best and worst, and how their capacity for doing their best can be maximized by planning, studying, and even experimenting.

If this sounds like an exploration into the outer reaches of what Alfred Conard calls "macrojustice,"[2] that is what is intended. The problem involves examining the respectable body of facts and insights accumulated about trial and appellate courts and their problems after almost a generation of energetic effort in judicial administration. Such an examination will suggest a number of steps that might directly improve the courts' capabilities to deal with problems that may face them in coming years.

The problem of court reform also must involve enlarging our perspectives on the social function of managing and resolving legal disputes by diverse systems and instruments. The most visible of these systems is the one by which judges and jurors fashion justice, with help from others—the court system. Courts, however, do not have a monopoly on the business of delivering justice in affrays that involve

---

2 Conard, *Macrojustice: A Systematic Approach to Conflict Resolution*, 5 GA. L. REV. 415, 420 (1971). Conard defines "macrojustice" as "a way of thinking about how various legal problems such as negligence law, larceny law, fair housing laws, or pretrial conference requirements operate in their total consequences."

legal conflict.[3] Those who would reform the judicial system must also canvass the means and tribunals other than courts available for managing legal disputes.

Administrative agencies using quasi-judicial processes, arbitrators, and perhaps even college disciplinary tribunals rely on court-type proceedings. Presumably other entities engaged in dispensing justice to people asserting legal claims do not. For example, court-type hearings are not employed by many of the executive bureaus that pass on license applications, social security benefit claims, tax adjustments, immigration entry permits, and countless other types of claimed rights. In many of those situations, the processes could be converted to trial-type adversary hearings, and sometimes they are. The point is, whatever their particular processes, they are engaged in passing on law-based claims and in that sense are doing something akin to what courts do in resolving disputes.

My uneasiness about throwing all our problems to the judges for decision does not trace to a lack of admiration for judges. On the contrary, I have the highest esteem for jurists as a breed. Holding a bias in favor of courts has not in recent years been a heavy cross to bear, even allowing for the dismaying scandals that have touched state courts in Oklahoma, Illinois, and New York, and the unhappy Fortas episode in the Supreme Court.[4] In the main the judges have acquitted themselves well as more and more of the society's sticky problems have gone their way.

Quite simply, my position is that the American system overemphasizes the use of trial-type court litigation. A pervasive question that confronts the architects of a modern justice system is whether some of the courts' work should be sloughed off to other agencies of government or to private groups or even converted to noncontentious form by rewriting the substantive rules to make clear when there is to be no contest. Awarding compensation without litigation is an example.[5]

The nature and the magnitude of growth of the judicial role are

---

3 See Rosenberg, *Frank Talk on Improving the Administration of Justice*, 47 TEXAS L. REV. 1029, 1030 (1969).

4 N.Y. Times, Mar. 24, 1972, at 1, col. 3; *id.*, Nov. 19, 1970, at 1, col. 1; *id.*, May 16, 1969, at 1, cols. 6, 8; *id.*, May 5, 1969, at 1, col. 6; *id.*, May 16, 1967, at 1, col. 5; *id.*, Nov. 5, 1966, at 1, col. 7; *id.*, Mar. 28, 1965, at 62, col. 3.

5 See Barry, *Compensation Without Litigation*, 37 AUSTL. L.J. 339, 343 (1964); Rosenberg, *Devising Procedures That Are Civil To Promote Justice That Is Civilized*, 69 MICH. L. REV. 797, 813-816 (1971).

important concepts to keep in view in thinking about how best to manage legal conflict in the years ahead. So are the society's premises about the whole problem of resolving legal disputes in court.

II. IMPROVING COURTS' CAPABILITIES

The architects of modern court structures and the improvers of judicial processes must try to develop a system of adjudication that is high in product quality and systemic efficiency, and low in stress and conflict. Whenever possible, the ideal system would provide justice without contention. When contention is unavoidable, the system should assure fairness and civility in the processes by which it is conducted. Using softer pedals and other instruments in orchestrating the choruses of legal disputation will mark a very considerable shift from present emphasis.

The term "polycentric" has been applied to some of the new types of controversies involving complex, technical issues, affecting the interests of large groups of people, presenting the possibility of numerous potential outcomes, and radiating wide direct consequences.[6] The new types of disputes implicating such large social issues as educational finance, siting of nuclear power plants, and redistricting of governmental units to meet one-man-one-vote requirements are steadily increasing in numbers. Their growing frequency invites scrutiny of the strengths and limits of the judicial process in dealing with these polycentric controversies.

Essentially, the matter boils down to how well the trial-type adversarial hearing functions when the court has to determine vastly ramified and technical fact questions[7] and how much help existing judicial mechanisms give courts in formulating serviceable legal norms in large polycentric disputes. The conclusion that emerges is that in planning courts for tomorrow we ought to build in new capabilities to deal with both aspects of these problems. Traditional court cases did not fore-

---

[6] *See* L. Fuller, The Forms and Limits of Adjudication 36 (unpublished mimeo); B. Boyer, A Re-Evaluation of Administrative Trial-Type Hearings for Resolving Complex Scientific and Economic Issues 23 (Staff Report to the Chairman of the Administrative Conference of the United States, December 1, 1971).

[7] Professor Boyer has written a penetrating paper on the efficacy of adversarial, trial-type proceedings in deciding "polycentric" issues. *See* Boyer, *supra* note 6, at 23-32. He sets forth three basic criteria for evaluating a procedural system: accuracy, efficiency, and acceptability. For accuracy in cases involving scientific issues, trial-type hearings are unsatisfactory since "they may bias decisionmaking in favor of a legalistic result when a greater reliance on scientific methods would be appropriate." *Id.* at 24. A second failing of trial-type procedures in deciding polycentric issues is their high cost, a mark of inefficiency. In respect to acceptability, trial-type procedures do better. They limit bureaucratic power and allow citizens direct participation in the decision of issues affecting them.

warn of the need for the retooling that is needed, as brief reflection will show.

Traditionally, a court decision has been triggered by a controversy, arising out of a past transaction, that has ripened sufficiently for judicial determination. With *stare decisis* at work, bygone disputes cast shadows ahead, and the court's judgment becomes a norm for the future. The typical court adjudication is "bipolar," commanding that plaintiff win or plaintiff lose, and if the former, how much. Cases that involve the issue of where needed nuclear reactors will be sited, or how large they need be, do not precisely fit that mold. Neither do cases determining whether school districts' cross-busing plans meet the requirements of law; or where boundary lines will have to be drawn to satisfy one-man-one-vote requirements. Standard proof-taking methods, designed to determine as a yes or no matter whether the defendant's car ran a red light two years ago, are basically inappropriate to issues of that type.

The California school-financing decision, *Serrano v. Priest*,[8] is an example of a controversy in which the courts were not equipped to know and the litigants were doubtless not motivated or able to produce the information the courts needed to render judgment about the complex of socio-economic issues lurking in the case. The *Serrano* decision underlines the point that if courts in the future are to deal competently with polycentric issues of that scale, they will have to be equipped with better fact-gathering capability and with more flexible remedial processes. The California Supreme Court reasoned that the system of financing public schools invidiously discriminated against poor people and denied them equal protection of the laws by making the quality of a child's education dependent on the wealth of the district the child happened to live in.

That much of the story shows the courts at their best in resolving disputes: applying a principle of law to a controverted claim of entitlement, identifying the winner on the point at issue, and explaining the reason. In *Serrano* the point was fiscal evenhandedness. Educational disparities cannot be justified as reflecting the varying wealth of school districts.

The rest of the story, however, demonstrates the weakness of courts in deciding polycentric issues that send out major shock waves affecting tax structures and school systems. The California Supreme Court could discern constitutional inequality in school support by property taxation, but it could not devise remedies. It had to leave

---

[8] 5 Cal. 3d 584, 487 P.2d 1241, 96 Cal. Rptr. 601 (1971).

the remedy question to other agencies of government, at least for the time being. It also left a legacy of uncertainties overhanging. For example, the court ignored the question of whether a state's failure to equalize school tax rates violates the equal protection clause.[9] Moreover, the decision is unclear as to whether the Constitution requires mandatory equal school spending per capita. None of the post-*Serrano* cases require that the legislature adopt one measure rather than another.

Through all the uncertainties, one plain imperative emerges. The voting-districting cases, the school-financing cases, the welfare-benefits cases, the school racial balance cases, and many others present a problem pattern which court system planners must take into account. All those cases require complex and massive piles of data as predicates for decision. Neither the information resources, nor the rules for its acquisition and presentation in court, nor present-day decision technologies are up to the demands of problems of that type.

Courts clearly lack an institutional capacity to obtain information they need if they are to dispose wisely of complex controversies involving ramified, technical information.[10] The parties are principally interested in winning the case, not in solving a cluster of thorny collateral problems that intertwine with the one in which they are enmeshed. Probably they lack either means or motive to go beyond the immediate needs of their own situation. They are unlikely to provide the court with the types of data an alert legislative committee would insist upon if at work on the same problem. *Amici* are not prone to take up the slack, for their interests are also likely to be confined to slices of the problem.

As for the courts themselves generating the essential information, it is unrealistic to count on a court's being able to anticipate the varied, changing needs for sophisticated data it will encounter. What *is* realistic, and even imperative, is that we think about building into court systems flexible and responsive capabilities for handling the new types of polycentric controversies and the massive issues calling for social data that are coming into court.

One helpful step would be to magnify courts' judicial notice

---

9 *See* N.Y. Times, Jan. 10, 1972, § E (annual education review), at 26, cols. 6, 10, tracing the spread of the *Serrano* principle into other court decisions, notably in Texas, Rodriguez v. San Antonio Independent School Dist., 337 F. Supp. 280 (W.D. Tex. 1971), *prob. juris. noted*, 40 U.S.L.W. 3576 (U.S. June 7, 1972), and Minnesota, Van Dusartz v. Hatfield, 334 F. Supp. 870 (D. Minn. 1971), and analyzing possible impacts on the financial bases of education in this country.

10 The judicial system "is intellectually the weakest part of our government. It has the least opportunity to get adequate information on the issues which it has to decide." M. COHEN, AMERICAN THOUGHT: A CRITICAL SKETCH 164 (1954).

capacity. A procedure should be fashioned to enable the courts to overcome their current inability to obtain and exploit information that informed persons would regard as essential to a sound resolution of complex "pluralegal" disputes.

A complementary need is to create an information facility from which courts can draw social data, not exclusively, but to supplement evidence from the litigants. Whether it be by resurrecting, revamping, and renaming Cardozo's virtually untried concept of a Ministry of Justice, or by creating some other institutional apparatus, the stark reality is that courts need new resources to cope with their novel problems. When decision turns not on reconstituting probabilities as to past events but upon projections of the social impact of practical alternative courses, courts should not continue to operate by hunch or by the fortuity of what litigants may turn up and present in evidence.

The most attractive approach is to create a new public agency— probably at the national level. It might be a consortium of scholars and scientists drawn from the Library of Congress, the National Institutes of Health, the National Science Foundation, the National Endowment for the Humanities, and other entities. Its mission would be to receive and catalog social impact studies that deserve judicial or legislative attention. The criteria for determining whether a study qualifies for a mark of approval would not be agreement or disagreement with its content or recommendations, but only a finding that its design and methodology fall within the range of accepted standards of scientific inquiry. These standards would be akin to "standard accounting principles" in financial matters. Courts would be free to take judicial notice of studies found methodologically acceptable, of course giving proper notification to the parties and perhaps to the *amici curiae*. Use of information found methodologically acceptable would in no way foreclose resort to other data; it would merely assure that a public agency would serve as a resource when needed.

As to the second failing dramatized by the *Serrano* line of decisions, courts need to be provided with a more flexible set of remedial options. Perhaps as equity courts they inherently possess the power to hold open judgments until legislatures act, but it would be helpful if both the power and the range of options were spelled out explicitly.

III. Changing Litigation Incentives and Rewards

Another neglected road to improving the quality of civil litigation is to find incentives for litigants to move toward settlement. Signs have recently appeared that a few steps have been taken at last to put us on that road, particularly in programs attempting to depolarize the adversarial process in scattered areas of civil disputes.

Personal injury cases and their present-day bargaining dynamics offer one example of the potential benefits of a more rational settlement process. Physical injury torts account for at least one-fourth of the energy output of major trial courts in the country.[11] In Texas there were about 26,000 personal injury cases on the District Court dockets on January 1, 1970, and the courts took in an additional 19,000 during the next 12 months.[12] Some constructive way of leading a portion of those suits to happy endings without court intervention would make a significant dent in the workload. A possible method to do that would be to change the reward system.

Today the ritual of disputation in typical automobile injury cases unfolds under principles and practices that are truly absurd. Their dominant theme is that neither side may approach within shouting distance of the other lest this be taken as a sign of weakness. These are the operating rules:

Rule 1. If you are plaintiff, make an extremely high and unrealistic demand to convince the insurance company either that you are morally certain you have suffered a catastrophic injury or else that you are out of your mind—in either event, signaling trouble ahead for the insurance company. If you are defendant, make an offer that is equally wild on the low side.

Rule 2. Make concessions that move your position toward your adversary's with the same generous alacrity you would show if asked to cut off your right hand.

Rule 3. Recognize that you can never retract a less extreme demand or offer, and furiously resist any impulse to be the first to be reasonable. Make the other side do all the reasonable yielding. Give a grudging inch only after you get a yard.

Rule 4. A good time to start trying to dispose of the case for what you believe it is actually worth is on the eve of trial, or just before or just after the jury is chosen. A particular reason for keeping a safe distance between what you say and what you believe is your awareness that when the case goes to court, the judge may try to get you to split the difference. Therefore, keep a comfortable distance to split.

---

11 *See* THE ADMINISTRATIVE BOARD OF THE JUDICIAL CONFERENCE OF THE STATE OF NEW YORK, SEVENTEENTH ANNUAL REPORT App. A, at A70, Table 7 (July 1, 1970-June 30, 1971). Approximately 41% of the 86,026 cases noticed for trial in the New York Supreme Court involved claims for personal injury. The majority of these (more than 25,000) were traffic injuries.

12 42 TEXAS CIVIL JUDICIAL COUNCIL ANN. REP. 167 (1970).

Rule 5. Pay no attention to what all this may do to the court's functioning or its capacity to deal with its caseload. Your job is to do the best you can by your client. If this ritual fire dance method is the way, do it!

These observations may seem flippant. They are not intended to be. An impressive body of evidence shows they are both accurate and grave. Careful field investigations and experimental studies confirm that this charade goes on as a regular, widespread practice. The result is heavy attrition on the courts' energies, not only in adjudicating cases that might have been settled, but in conducting bargaining sessions. This is a form of waste that will not yield to revamped court structures, streamlined procedures or modern administration. But it can be significantly reduced.

The general strategy I propose as a positive step is to modify the rewards and incentives to lawyers and litigants engaged in the haggling process I have depicted, basically to encourage them not to cling to polarized positions. One way this might be done can be quickly outlined. At the start the adversaries would be told that they are to engage in settlement discussions and that their bargaining will culminate neither in a judge-directed settlement conference nor in a climactic trial, but in an ending of an entirely different kind: the side will win which has presented as its final demand or offer an amount that is closer than the opposing party's figure to a prospective award that will be made in the case by an impartial adjudicator.

Notice how this rule changes the trading incentives and dynamics in a hypothetical case. When the parties have finished bargaining, the plaintiff's lowest demand—say, $10,000—is put in a sealed envelope. The same is done with the defendant's highest offer—for example, $6,000. Both envelopes are put aside while the impartial adjudicator takes proof—to the extent possible, in the form of written testimony and documents. (Assume here that liability is not in issue.) The adjudicator records his figure, representing his view of what the claim is fairly worth—for example, $7,500.

The adjudicator then opens the two sealed envelopes, compares the plaintiff's demand and the defendant's offer with his own estimate, and awards the amount that came closer to his figure. In the supposed case, the award would be the defendant's offer of $6,000.

A procedure of this sort would completely alter the bargaining dynamics in unliquidated damage cases. The way to win would be to get "inside" one's opponent's bid—that is, to come closer to the amount a fair-minded, neutral person would supposedly fix as the damages due. In that setting a plaintiff who lowers his opening high demand will be moving toward a winning position rather than bidding against himself; the converse will be true for the defendant. In the final stages of the bidding, if not sooner, each side would have a strong incentive to move toward the "fair" award in prospect. Extremism in the trading process would serve no purpose and at the end would be self-defeating. The built-in impulse for both sides to move toward each other as they bargained might often result in closing the gap to an amount so narrow that continuing the litigation would be uneconomical.

Such a process might achieve settlements that are both fair and fast, sparing litigants, particularly poorer ones, the agony of indecision that delayed, crowded courts inflict upon suitors. Not at all incidentally, the courts themselves would be spared wasted energy in proportion to the success of the depolarization program.

Of course there would be problems. A voluntary program would probably encounter the twin hazards of any invitation to the bar to try something new in live cases. One danger is the reaction: "If my good friend Barry P. Mergl wants the procedure for his client, it can't be any good for mine." The other is the response: "No, thanks! If I were to get clobbered, how would I explain it to the client and my partners?" Furthermore, a compulsory program would have to be squared with the right to jury trial. Still, in other contexts ingenuity has devised lawful ways of loosening the grip of troublesome procedures. There is no reason to despair here, if willing minds take up the challenge.

An analogous suggestion has been put forward by the Administration under the name "final offer selection" to end labor disputes that paralyze transportation.[13] The essence of the proposal is that in national emergency labor disputes at a prescribed stage of the procedures the two sides would be required to submit final offers. If deadlock persisted through succeeding stages, an appointed board would decide which offer, without alteration, would be mandated as the collective agreement between the parties. Differences between the "final offer selection" proposal and the depolarization incentives outlined a moment ago are readily apparent. The feature they share, and the point to drive home in this cursory treatment of a complicated idea, is that both proposals aim to reward the parties for seeking

---

[13] Harlan, *An Answer to "National Emergency" Transportation Strikes*, 58 A.B.A.J. 26 (1972).

common ground near the center of the arena, rather than circling each other warily and unyieldingly at unbridgeable distances.

The law and law reformers are probably excessively preoccupied with trying to make good things happen by threatening that otherwise bad things will happen. They ought to look harder for carrots and lavish some benign neglect on sticks. Although rewards may be more difficult to devise than penalties, they are very likely worth the trouble.

IV. NONJUDICIAL WAYS OF MANAGING LEGAL DISPUTES

Courts generally have a good reputation as dispute resolvers—so good that the boom in their business has reached the dimensions of an explosion. There is no mystery about the underlying dynamics and motivations involved in this activity. Someone thinks another person or the government has infringed an entitlement that is grounded in a legal right and the battle is on. The "right" relied upon may be one that has become well settled by the time of suit; it may be based upon a constitution, a statute, or a court decision. Or it may be an inchoate right that no one knows for certain exists until a litigant asserts it and is vindicated.

A.   Changes in Law To Make the Fight No-Contest

Suing in court is quite obviously not the only way to create or vindicate entitlements, or to manage disputes about their existence, scope, and applicability. A legislature may remove the core of conflict from an established type of dispute by the simple expedient of defining the right in such absolute terms that it can no longer be seriously challenged. For instance, a law that gives a passenger injured in an auto accident an absolute "no-fault" right to recover economic loss makes it needless to argue whether the driver or anyone else was negligent in causing the injury.

A similar approach could be adopted to liquidate contention over how much the victim's loss is worth. A flat sum might be legislatively prescribed for each injured victim, regardless of how much he or she suffered in fact. Alternatively, the legislature might install a workmen's compensation type of system, keying loss benefits to the specific type of injury sustained.[14]

---

14 *See* SPECIAL COMMITTEE ON AUTOMOBILE INSURANCE PLANS, ASSOCIATION OF THE BAR OF THE CITY OF NEW YORK. THE "NO-FAULT" PRINCIPLE 6 (1972).

This legislative route to eliminating contentious issues by rewriting norms has been much used in recent years—to create strict liability for product failure,[15] to adopt no-fault predicates for relief in automobile[16] or marital smashups,[17] to decriminalize certain sumptuary offenses.[18] The prospect is that this route will be used even more in years ahead. This development has most important implications in planning new court structures and procedures, for very likely the classes of controversy departing from the courts will be replaced by others that will make radically different types of demands upon the judicial process.

B. Arbitration and "Fair Insurance Settlement Tribunals"

A second nonjudicial approach to managing disputes is to leave the underlying substantive rules intact, but reroute the disputes into other adjudicative systems. One of the others is arbitration, which has had a remarkable growth in a brief span of years. Voluntary arbitrations in labor-management relations reportedly have increased in five years from 4,437 to 6,658 annually.[19] Including commercial and "human relations" disputes, the American Arbitration Association reports a rise from 14,763 to 22,459 arbitrations in the same period.[20]

Most arbitrated disputes undoubtedly turn on applications of well-accepted legal norms. Occasionally some reveal that arbitration law has growing pains akin to those experienced by the law in courts. One recent arbitration involved the firing of a male employee by a plant in which there were forty male and seven hundred female employees. He was discharged after he read aloud in the company's cafeteria a few spicy passages from love letters written to him by a

15 *Cf.* Uniform Commercial Code § 2-314, judicially interpreted as imposing strict liability on sellers for breach of implied warranty of fitness. Newmark v. Gimbel's, Inc., 54 N.J. 585, 258 A.2d 697 (1969).

16 *See* Del. Code Ann. tit. 21, § 2118 (1953); Mass. Gen. Laws Ann. ch. 90, §§ 34A, 34D, 34M, 34N (1969), *as amended*, (Supp. 1972), and ch. 231, § 6D (1959), *as amended*, (Supp. 1972); N.Y. Sen. 8000, 195th Sess. (1972). *Cf.* Ill. Ins. Code art. 35, §§ 1065.150-.163 (Supp. 1972); Ore. Laws 1971, H.B. 1300, *amending* Ore. Rev. Stat. § 731.418 (1969), and § 743.786 (1967).

17 *Cf.* Alas. Stat. § 09.55.110(5)(c) (1962); N.M. Stat. Ann. § 22-7-1(8) (1953); Okla. Stat. tit. 12, § 1271 (1961); V.I. Code Ann. tit. 16, § 104(a)(8) (1964). *See also* N.Y. Dom. Rel. Law. §§ 170(5), (6) (McKinney 1971).

18 *See* Fla. Stat. § 396.012 *et seq.* (1972 Supp.) (Florida Comprehensive Alcoholism Prevention, Control and Treatment Act); Kadish, *The Crisis of Overcriminalization*, 7 Am. Crim. L.Q. 17 (1968); Packer, *The Aims of the Criminal Law Revisited: A Plea for a New Look at "Substantive Due Process,"* 44 S. Cal. L. Rev. 490 (1971). *Cf.* Remington, *The Limits and Possibilities of the Criminal Law*, 43 Notre Dame Law. 865 (1968).

19 N.Y. Times, Mar. 12, 1972, at 70, cols. 1, 2.

20 *Id.*

woman employee who had later jilted him.[21] Free speech or cause for firing? That is quite a question to submit to labor arbitration.

What attributes of the arbitration process account for its rising popularity in competition with courts? Frequently mentioned virtues are its emancipation from the rules of evidence,[22] the lack of necessity to justify an award by reasons properly based upon the law and proof,[23] and nonappealability of the award.[24] Ironically, these are the opposites of the very attributes of court justice that cause it to be held in such high esteem.

How is it that the courts' strengths become faults in the view of those who seek out the arbitration process? Is it simply that all those prized virtues of court justice pale into inconsequentiality when matched against the cheaper, quicker, and more convenient schedules arbitration makes available? How can first-round finality be so estimable a feature of arbitration when a guaranteed second review by appeal is so warmly praised as a feature of court litigation?

A study of these and similar paradoxes in the coprosperity sphere experienced by the arbitral and court processes is long overdue. The study could teach us much about what the users of arbitration regard as particular blemishes in court processes. An inquiry is peculiarly timely now because of the continuing trend toward mandatory arbitration of court-commenced suits in such major states as Pennsylvania and New York and in the city of Cleveland. Recently California has begun a serious investigation into compulsory arbitration of court-initiated suits.[25] Other states are showing signs of interest.

Mandatory arbitration, compelled by law without regard to the parties' wishes, was largely a Philadelphia phenomenon from the mid-1950's until little over a year ago. It had existed throughout the Commonwealth of Pennsylvania, but the first large rise in its use occurred when small suits filed in Philadelphia Municipal Court were diverted to volunteer three-lawyer panels. Initially, the monetary limit

---

21 *Id.*

22 Sarpy, *Arbitration as a Means of Reducing Court Congestion,* 41 Notre Dame Law. 182, 188, 190 (1965); Schiffer, *Arbitrate or Litigate? A Question for Credit Executives,* 20 Arb. J. (N.S.) 49, 50-51 (1965).

23 *An Outline of Procedure Under the New York Arbitration Law,* 20 Arb. J. (N.S.) 73, 88 (1965).

24 *See* McDermott, *Arbitrability: The Courts Versus the Arbitrator,* 23 Arb. J. (N.S.) 18, 19 (1968); Schiffer, *supra* note 22, at 51.

25 Judicial Council of California, Arbitration Study. The authority of the California Judicial Council is based on Cal. Const. art. 6, § 6.

on divertible cases was $2,000; for a long time it was $3,000; and recently it has been raised to $10,000.

In New York, after a one-year preview in Rochester, the ceiling was raised from $3,000 to $4,000. The system has also spread to the Bronx.[26]

To save compulsory arbitration procedures from constitutional attack for depriving litigants of the right to trial by jury, the rules provide that after the arbitration a dissatisfied party may get a trial *de novo*. As long as the claim ceilings were low and awards averaged only a few hundred dollars, the percentage of *de novo* trials was also low. Whether the compulsory arbitration plan will continue to keep cases out of court now that $10,000 claims are being arbitrated remains to be seen. If enough of the large claims return to court following an arbitration award because one side finds it unsatisfactory, the system will probably collapse, for the consequence would be a double trial in the returning cases, with the attendant waste of effort for the lawyers who serve as counsel as well as for those who serve as arbitrators.[27]

Another procedure, recently proposed in New York, for out-of-court handling of adversary contests has immense potential because it has been coupled to the so-called Gordon Plan of no-fault auto injury reparation.[28] As no-fault statutes spread across the country, the idea put forward in New York will be watched very carefully by states that look upon no-fault as a way of moving large numbers of accident cases out of the courts. The Gordon bill proposes setting up a noncourt agency called the "Fair Insurance Settlement Tribunal" —FIST for short. FIST might have to hear very substantial claims, because the stakes in New York under the no-fault bill can run very high. For example, an insurance company might dispute the victim's contention that he had been injured by a skidding auto instead of a slippery bathtub or an oil-slick in the garage. The company might deny the injuries were as disabling as claimed or that the hospital stay was connected with a traffic accident instead of an irritated gall bladder.

---

26 N.Y. JUDICIARY LAW § 213(8) (McKinney Supp. 1971); N.Y. CODES, RULES AND REGULATIONS tit. 22, pt. 28 (1971).

27 *See* Rosenberg, *Court Congestion: Status, Causes, and Proposed Remedies,* in THE COURTS, THE PUBLIC, AND THE LAW EXPLOSION 29, 52 (H. Jones ed. 1965); Rosenberg & Schubin, *Trial by Lawyer: Compulsory Arbitration of Small Claims in Pennsylvania,* 74 HARV. L. REV. 448, 451 (1961).

Arbitrators are paid, but at rates it would be sheerest hyperbole to call modest—at least $35 a hearing.

28 N.Y. Sen. 8000, 195th Sess. (1972).

These positions would be worth asserting if the company stood a fair chance of making them stick.

The Gordon Plan would pay no-fault benefits of up to $50,000 for medical and hospital costs, up to almost $30,000 for lost earnings (with a ceiling of $9,600 a year tax-free), up to nearly $10,000 for miscellaneous losses related to bodily injury, and up to $5,000 in property damage (not including damage to a vehicle). Although the detailed procedures for FIST have not yet been drawn up, it seems quite likely that many claimants and insurers will have strong motive to take unsatisfactory FIST determinations back to court. Can honest lawyerly ingenuity somehow devise incentives to prevent the litigants from returning to burden the judicial system after being pummeled by FIST?

The ingenuity must be honorable, not merely clever. Otherwise the custodians of justice will be found doing by subterfuge what they could not or would not do openly. This is not the way to enhance public confidence in the fairness of the system of justice. Perhaps a fair way can be devised to combine the idea suggested earlier for stimulating settlements by rewarding moderation in bargaining with innovative procedures for resolving controversies over amounts of benefits due under no-fault plans. While Illinois, Oregon, and Delaware make use of arbitration in one way or another in connection with their auto injury reparation plans,[29] the much higher scale of benefits in the New York plan and the idea of the settlement tribunals for no-fault claims seem to be natural prospects for procedural mating.

V.   ADMINISTRATION OF CRIMINAL JUSTICE:
HINTS OF SPECIAL PROBLEMS

An unmistakable movement in the administration of criminal justice today is toward prompt trials. The desirability of promptness is proclaimed in the United States Constitution and endorsed by virtually everyone. Speedy judgments are due both the accused and the society. This aspiration is apparently one of the most widely shared viewpoints in the whole panorama of court justice.

In New York, the authorities have adopted rules that set limits on permissible detention time of accused persons: unless charged with homicide, anyone taken into custody must be released with or without

---

29 DEL. CODE ANN. tit. 21, § 2118(4)(i) (1971); ILL. INS. CODE art. 35, §§ 1065.155, 1065.159 (Supp. 1972); ORE. REV. STAT. § 743.792(1)(a) (1967).

money bail within 90 days after arrest if he has not been tried by then; and if he is not brought to actual trial in six months, the charges must be dismissed altogether.[30]

Quite obviously, prompt trial rules can only be enforced if adequate resources exist—adequate courts, defense lawyers, prosecutors, supporting personnel, and administrative capabilities. As pressure to make the authorities try-or-say-good-bye to the criminally accused spreads, those facing trial will perhaps try to gain freedom by running out the time limits instead of bargaining for a reduced plea or sentence, as now happens in as many as 95 percent of the charges. This will present serious problems to a state embracing the prompt trial rules. The problems must be anticipated, and preparations made to handle them. Stand-by authority to create auxiliary courtrooms and to draw upon reserves of lawyer and other personnel will be essential. The period of critical shock from introduction of prompt trial rules can be a short one if the right plans are made and implemented. This prediction rests upon a series of assumptions that requires stating.

1. Much of the present delay in bringing criminal cases to trial is not opposed by the accused persons or their counsel,[31] particularly when the defendant is out on bail. A federal judge told me not long ago that many indigents accused of crime in his court refuse legal aid attorneys, preferring lawyers whom they must hire and pay. Since these defendants are by definition unmoneyed, they are in effect compelling themselves to develop funds suddenly—often nocturnally. They do this because a paid lawyer will work harder and more effectively to delay trial. For a defendant with dim prospects of acquittal, trial delayed is doom deferred, and sometimes averted completely.

2. The practice of plea-bargaining that accounts for anywhere from 50 percent to 95 percent of the guilty judgments entered around the country is not, as some argue, in main part a mockery of due process or bitterly opposed by defendants.[32] To be sure, the process

---

30 N.Y. Codes, Rules and Regulations tit. 22, §§ 29.1-.7 (1971). Time used by defendants for motions or continuances is not counted as part of these limited periods.

31 In a recent felony trial involving twin brothers as defendants, news accounts report that one arose to plead for more time to prepare a defense. The court noted that the prosecution had been ready for 10 months, that defendants had three times dismissed lawyers, had been heard on pretrial motions, and admonished the defendants to get on with the defense. To this the vocal defendant reportedly replied: "It is the right of the accused to a speedy trial. We waive that right. What we want is a fair trial." *See* N.Y. Times, Mar. 15, 1972, at 51, col. 3.

See also Hedgepeth v. United States, 364 F.2d 684, 688 (D.C. Cir. 1966); United States *ex rel.* Von Cseh v. Fay, 313 F.2d 620, 623 (2d Cir. 1963); Comment, *The Convict's Right to a Speedy Trial*, 61 J. Crim. L.C. & P.S. 352, 361 (1970).

32 *See* Gentile, *Fair Bargains and Accurate Pleas*, 49 B.U.L. Rev. 514, 523 (1969): "[T]he

must be made visible and subjected to decent, agreed-on rules and precautions of the kind being proposed by capable committees of the A.B.A. and the Judicial Conference of the United States, among others. But I reject as unsupported and self-defeating the submission that plea bargaining is by its very nature so suspect a practice that it must be declared unconstitutional or illegal if large numbers of cases are disposed of by pleas.

An able judge has advanced the view that "the Supreme Court might be persuaded to rule in an appropriate case that pleas of guilty would be the result of undue influence whenever their rate exceeded 90 or 95 percent of all convictions in a particular court. . . ."[33] The author, Judge Harold Greene, asserts that when guilty pleas reach so high a proportion of dispositions, fairness is affronted and constitutional due process is reduced to tokenism. He guesses that for $150,000,000 a year we could reclaim our virtue by expanding courts, the number of judges, and the other physical components of the judicial system. He may be right, yet there are certainly some who would argue that the $150,000,000 per year should be put into more hospitals before we put them into more court facilities and that we need more doctors at least as much as more prosecutors or defenders.

Besides, it is not at all clear that more money will buy happiness in criminal justice if we pour it into the same rat-holes we have been filling year-in, year-out. The New York City Criminal Justice Coordinating Council, fresh from spending $18 million last year to improve administration of criminal justice, recently came out strongly against the pour-on-dollars approach. According to news accounts

> the report repeatedly emphasized that the traditional answer of simply providing the courts with additional money was no longer acceptable.
> "It simply has not been established that more resources are the principal answer to court problems," the report said. "Without steps to improve efficiency, still further major commitment of scarce resources cannot be justified."[34]

3. My final assumption is exposed by now. Some observers tend to overvalue the full-dress trial with its exquisite, drawn-out *voir dire* in selecting a jury, its meticulous attention to all the venerable rules

---

principal object of the defendant is to obtain leniency . . . ." *See also* D. NEWMAN, CONVICTION: THE DETERMINATION OF GUILT OR INNOCENCE WITHOUT TRIAL 97 (1966); Note, *Plea Bargaining—Justice Off the Record*, 9 WASHBURN L.J. 430, 433 (1970); 46 CHI.-KENT L. REV. 116, 117, 120-22 (1969).

[33] Greene, *Court Reform: What Purpose?*, 58 A.B.A.J. 247, 250 (1972).
[34] N.Y. Times, Mar. 12, 1972, at 65, cols. 1, 2.

of evidence, examination and cross-examination, summings-up and instructions, post-trial motions and appeals,[35] and its wide opportunities for collateral attacks. This is no doubt virtuous and a tribute to civilized compassion for the least among us. But it is not necessary to have it happen that way in every case or in some fixed percentage of the cases to assure fairness and decency in the system of criminal justice. "Trial procedure is not the only fair procedure."[36]

The essential attributes of an acceptable non-trial system of procedures are that the process be known and open and that pleas of guilty be entered knowingly and understandingly, with counsel available. If that is done, our $150,000,000 a year, instead of forcing a quota of full-dress criminal trials, could be used for schools, narcotics control, health care, and environmental cleansing. If these areas have no need for them, the funds can be invested in correcting our correction system.

In civil litigation, wise lawyers often say that a bad settlement is better than a good trial outcome. I do not suggest this is always or generally true in criminal litigation; but neither is it true that happiness is a thing called full-scale trial or that the fairness of the criminal process comes under a cloud unless a fixed quota of trials is held.

VI. Conclusions and Recommendations

Having disclaimed at the start any intention to detail panaceas for healthy courts, I nevertheless end by assuring that there is a set of prescriptions for improving the administration of justice. I put to one side such matters as modernization of procedural rules and reduction of the jury to six members. Both are good proposals and amply discussed in the literature.

The imperatives I want to recommend are not doses of "do's" and "don'ts," but broader axioms and saws such as those one might find in *Poor Roscoe Pound's Almanac,* if he had written one and it were updated. For example:

1. As Pound said, justice is a compound of men and machinery in which the men count more than the mechanisms. The surest recipe for good judgments is good judges; and the surest prescription for well-managed courts is capable judges concerned with administration.

2. Good men are hard to find, especially considering that the

---

[35] *Cf.* Greene, *supra* note 33, at 248.
[36] *Cf.* K. Davis, Administrative Law Treatise § 7.16, at 358, 359 (1970 Supp.).

qualities that make good judges are highly subtle, subjective, and hard to measure before they put on the black robe.[37] After that they sometimes remove all doubt. But precisely because of the difficulty of deciding which of a host of reputable lawyers is peculiarly qualified to be a judge, the process of selection becomes especially important. This points strongly toward a merit selection process in which considerations other than fitness are disregarded.

3. Flexibility must be built into a modern court system to give it the capacity to adjust to changes in the volume, mix, or demands of its incoming workload.

4. Access to internal information is essential. The court system must have the means of knowing promptly the dimensions of its incoming workload, the state of its calendar, and statistical data on trends in the major classes of cases of which it must dispose. Predictive data are essential to a well-managed modern court.

5. Professional central administration can assure that the quantity of the court's work does not impair the quality of its workings.[38] Judges in many courts are already too busy with their adjudicatory and non-delegable administrative functions. They should have professional aides to get and interpret the information their busy courts vitally need.

6. Auditing by outsiders of court functioning ought to be provided on a regular basis. Evaluation cannot be left to insiders because of the well-known tendency of bureaucracy to find value in whatever it is doing. Serious evaluation involves challenging established routines, rather than accepting them as chiseled in the tablets.

7. Unification of trial courts to the greatest degree consistent with good sense and practicability is another goal worth considering. These words are deliberately voiced cautiously. In California today there is a considerable flap over whether Municipal Court judges, who are proposed to be absorbed in a unified court, shall be called "associate superior court judges" or by some other hyphenated title they do not warmly appreciate. The dilemma is to choose, on the one hand, to try to recruit lawyers of the highest professional standing to do what they regard as the least desirable judicial work, or, on the other hand,

---

[37] Rosenberg, *The Qualities of Justices—Are They Strainable?*, 44 TEXAS L. REV. 1063, 1065 (1966).

[38] *See* Brennan, *Effective Organization and Effective Administration for Today's Courts ... The Citizens' Responsibility*, 48 J. AM. JUD. SOC'Y 145, 146 (1965); McConnell, *The Administration of a State Court System*, 51 JUD. AM. JUD. SOC'Y 253 (1968).

to accept lawyers willing to sit as judges in "inferior" cases and assume they will also be qualified to sit in major cases. This is one of the kinds of problems that shows that complexity has a bright future.

8. Clean delineation of functions among trial courts and the various appellate courts in a multitiered system is needed. It makes little sense to have an intermediate appellate court and a supreme court that perform precisely the same functions, with the former merely a first draft copy of the highest court.

9. Diversified procedures should be considered for diverse types of cases in the same court. Not every civil case deserves full blown pre-trial processing. With Professor Charles A. Wright, I believe that, "A . . . promising area for the reformers is to reexamine the belief that all cases are to be handled by the same procedure."[39] Procedural rules and court processes tend to embrace the premise in dealing with varieties of cases that "all pigs is pigs" and equal pigs at that. In fact, different categories of actions behave differently in court. Strong statistical data will permit a court to give differential treatment to classes of cases that are destined for atypical court careers—such as trial, which is, of course, an atypical mode of disposition.

10. Intrasystem communication is a much neglected need.[40] A sense that the custodians of justice are concerned and caring can be transmitted to jurors (who are often disaffected by their experience in court), to lawyers, and to court personnel by moderate amounts of effort and ingenuity. The resulting lift in the morale of those having most to do with the courts will very likely inspire confidence in members of the public who have little to do with them.

11. Devising positive motivations of the type outlined in the suggestion about a new mode of bargaining that might depolarize disputes is strongly recommended. We need less emphasis on penalties and more upon rewards if we seek to encourage most strongly the actions by lawyers and litigants that the system wants most and needs most.

These are not trivial chores. They are also not sure cures. A German proverb goes: "Man errs so long as he strives." To err in trying to improve court justice is human; to strive is worthy of our professional trust.

---

[39] Wright, *Procedural Reform: Its Limitations and Its Future*, 1 Ga. L. Rev. 563, 581 (1967).

[40] *See* Meyer & Rosenberg, *Questions Juries Ask: Untapped Springs of Insight*, 55 J. Am. Jud. Soc'y 105 (1971).